BAPTIST HISTORICAL SOCIETY
2009

Printed by Tyndale Press (Lowestoft) Ltd

ISBN 978-0-903166-39-3

PROBING THE PAST

ACKNOWLEDGEMENTS

I would like to thank Professor John Briggs for his advice and encouragement and Mrs Faith Bowers for practical advice, as well as the Revd Dr Peter Shepherd, President, the Revd Stephen Copson, Hon. Secretary and the Committee of the Baptist Historical Society for their continuing support for this project.

Most of the research into printed and manuscript sources was carried out in the Angus Library, Regent's Park College, Oxford, for continued access to which as an Honorary Fellow of the Centre for Baptist History and Heritage since my retirement from the post of Librarian I should like to thank both past and present Principals, the Revd Professor Paul S. Fiddes and the Revd Dr Robert Ellis. I am grateful to the College Archivist, Dr Julian Lock, and my successors as Librarian, Mr Andrew Hudson and the Revd Emma Walsh, for their assistance. Above all, I would like to thank Mrs Sheila Wood, Assistant Librarian at Regent's Park College, to whom I dedicate this work, for her ongoing friendship and support.

I would also like to thank my husband Roger Mills, for his technical assistance.

Illustrations

Pictures marked (BMS) used courtesy of BMS World Mission (Baptist Missionary Society) archives, Angus Library at Regent's Park College, Oxford, UK. Many thanks to Suzanne Linnell for granting this permission.

Intute: screenshot of homepage on cover, logo, and quotations from website included by permission (dated 28/11/2008 and 13/03/2009). The site is to be redesigned during 2009, with a considerable change to the homepage.

The National Archives: logo (used solely for illustrative purposes) and quotations from website © Crown copyright 2009, reproduced with the permission of the National Archives (dated 10/12/2008).

The Baptist Historical Society logo used by permission of the President.

Illustration of *Sources for researching Nonconformists in Northamptonshire* included by permission of the author, Graham Ward.

The cover of *Pastors and People* is reproduced with permission of Queen's Road Baptist Church, Coventry, and Professor Clyde Binfield.

The remaining internal illustrations were taken by Mr R.A. Mills. Those of items belonging to Regent's Park College, Oxford (marked RPC) are used by permission of the Principal, the Revd Dr Robert Ellis. Those as noted of items within the Angus Library used by permission of the Angus Library, Regent's Park College, Oxford. Photograph of Angus Library bookshelf on the back cover taken by the Revd Professor Paul S. Fiddes, used with his permission and that of the Principal.

SUSAN J. MILLS

CONTENTS

(*Picture of BMS missionary Dr Timothy Richard in his study.* Ref. CH-P-10-15. Courtesy of BMS World Mission (Baptist Missionary Society) archives, Angus Library at Regent's Park College, Oxford, UK.

PROBING THE PAST

1. Introduction

This publication is aimed on the one hand at graduate, undergraduate and ministerial students at the outset of their research into Baptist history for a dissertation or extended essay and on the other at the private individual, whether local church historian, starting research into the history of his or her church, or biographical researcher into his or her family history. It updates its 1992 predecessor, *Sources for the study of Baptist history*[1], in a number of significant directions. In particular, the development of the Internet and the rapid expansion of resources available on the World Wide Web has led many students to think that they can find all the information and reference material that they require, accurately, via the Internet. This new edition aims to direct you both to what you *can* find on the Internet, but also to what you *cannot* find online, with regard to useful sources for the study of Baptist history. While many important library catalogues are available, and also easily searchable (not always the same thing) online, others are not, or are so only by means of expensive global gateways (like ESTC and OCLC WorldCat) not available in smaller institutions outside mainstream universities, such as many independent theological colleges, nor to the private researcher without access to large university or city libraries.

However, thanks to the Museums, Libraries and Archives Council's "Reference Online: subscription-based electronic services for English public libraries" agreement, many online reference tools, such as the Oxford Dictionary of National Biography, the Oxford Reference Online Premium Collection, Who's Who, the Times Digital Archive, and even sometimes OCLC WorldCat, may be accessible through your local public library membership number or in your local library. To find out which services are available in your area it is worth checking your county council library service website, or asking in your local public library. I hope to demonstrate what you can find on publicly available websites as well as what printed resources you can use by visiting a specialist library for Baptist or nonconformist history such as the Angus Library at Regent's Park College, Oxford or Dr Williams's Library in London. Nevertheless, I hope also to direct graduate, undergraduate and ministerial students just embarking on their first steps in research, who do have access via their universities to a wider range of resources, to websites and other electronic tools, which can help them to find useful academic material. I should also stress that this is largely UK, and even England, based, although some significant American and other worldwide websites and publications are included.

It is also worth remembering that the topic of "Baptist history" itself can be very wide and interdisciplinary in nature and I hope to provide examples of the different results achieved when thinking of our subject in terms of history, religion and theology, social studies or literature. The moral is always "think outside the box".

(Homepage of Intute as at February 2009, used by permission)

2. Search engines, gateways and general bibliographical resources

(a) Internet resources

When embarking on research on the Internet most people start with a general search engine such as Google. This is fine as a start, as long as you are as specific as possible with your search terms (see http://www.google.com/help/cheatsheet.html or try using Google Advanced Search, possibly with Google preferences set up), but it can bring back far too many possible sources of information, especially if the search is not limited in any way, and the sources which it comes up with may not be very authoritative. It will also not find resources on the "invisible or deep web", for which various strategies are advised, using either specialised search engines or subject gateways.

This is not the place to go into an extensive analysis of all the alternative search engines and gateways available on the Internet, or the various strategies to adopt when using them: see http://www.philb.com/whichengine.htm for

"What is the best resource to make use of?"

in answer to

"What do you need to find? what do you already know?".

It is also a good idea to compare search engines by doing a search in Google and comparing the results with those from another search engine such as http://www.exalead.co.uk./search, or by searching for material relevant to you in Google Scholar http://scholar.google.co.uk and comparing the results for your subject area with those from some of the subscription services mentioned below (if you have access to a university library service with such subscriptions). Make sure you have a look at the Advanced Scholar Search Tips before using Google Scholar.

(I found that when I searched for articles by a particular author who had sent me a list of his publications in a wide variety of journals including the *Baptist Quarterly*, several literary journals and *Women's Studies*, only Google Scholar retrieved eleven of the seventeen on a search of his name in combination with several alternative keywords common to many, but not all, of his articles. Those it did not retrieve either did not contain those keywords or were very recently published. *Web of Science* initially retrieved many hundreds of irrelevant articles by other authors of the same name, but when the search was refined sufficiently it found five of these articles. *British Humanities Index* retrieved only one. The moral is to be aware of the limitations of any one search service, particularly where the topic is interdisciplinary in nature, or where a relevant author contributes to a cross-section of journals, and to check which journals are in fact being indexed, although unfortunately with Google Scholar this is not possible.)

Another way to compare the results from selected search engines is to use http://www.thumbshots.org/Products/Thumbshots/Ranking.aspx, or with http://www.turboscout.com/ you can run the same search quickly across different search engines. Other metasearch engines include http://www.metacrawler.com and http://www.clusty.com.

(If you really want to go into internet searching in depth you may find Facet Publishing's *Going Beyond Google: The invisible web in learning and teaching*[2], which is aimed at librarians, of interest, or you might even wish to take the Open University's part-time short course "Beyond Google: working with information online"[3]: see http://www3.open.ac.uk/courses/bin/p12.dll?C01TU120)

Alternatively, in order to find the best databases for your particular topic you can use a general or subject specific gateway or web directory, although you need to check who is controlling the gateway and how it has been set up in order to assess the quality of the results it produces. For a scholarly overview and review of potentially useful websites it is a good idea to start with the general gateway Intute http://www.intute.ac.uk/.

[Logo reproduced with permission]

It describes itself thus:

"Intute is a free online service providing access to the very best
web resources for education and research. All material is
evaluated and selected by a network of subject specialists to
create the Intute database. With millions of resources available
on the Internet, it is difficult to find relevant and appropriate
material even if you have good search skills and use advanced
search engines. Issues of trust, quality, and search skills are
very real and significant concerns - particularly in a learning
context. Academics, teachers, students and researchers are
faced with a complex environment, with different routes into
numerous different resources, different user interfaces, search
mechanisms and authentication processes. The Intute database
makes it possible to discover the best and most relevant
resources in one easily accessible place. You can explore and
discover trusted information, assured that it has been evaluated
by specialists for its quality and relevance."[4]

Our subject is such that searching for resources in both the Historians
and the Religious Studies subject divisions of the Arts & Humanities
section is recommended, and if you are not familiar with Internet
searching in these fields you are advised to work through the Virtual
Training Suite in each of these subject areas before you start on your
research. (N.B. The site is to be redesigned during 2009, with the four
current subject groupings merged into one.) There you will find links
to websites which may be of use to you, which you can either access
immediately or, probably more usefully, place into a "Links basket"
which you can then either download or email to yourself before you
leave the Virtual Training Suite, so that you can examine them later at
your leisure and pick out the sites you think will be most helpful. The
VTS also includes useful guidelines on assessing the potential
reliability of websites and online documents found. Alternatively,
work through the "Internet Detective" at
http://www.vts.intute.ac.uk/detective/index.html, a free online tutorial
aimed at students in higher and further education, which "looks at the
critical thinking required when using the Internet for research and

offers practical advice on evaluating the quality of web sites"[5]. Some of the tips in this are extremely relevant and well worth adhering to.

A small selection of some of the most useful general bibliographical databases and online library catalogues, plus a few sites for searching archives, with some specific biographical sources and general guides, are given below. Unfortunately, there is no consistency to the methods of searching even different university and national library catalogues, nor of specifying an author's name, so it is worth taking time when you first access one of these to check its search tips or Help screens in order to maximise the efficiency of your searching. When searching for authors, particularly from earlier centuries, it is wise to check variant spellings of the name and alternative forenames and when searching by topic, subject index or keyword, it is also necessary to think of any possible synonyms for your terms, to use wildcards wherever offered and useful, and above all to remember that the word "Baptist" will retrieve an enormous number of churches dedicated to St. John the Baptist or articles about the saint himself!

WorldCat (OCLC) (institutional subscription required, but may be available in your local public library under the MLA "Reference Online" agreement)
http://www.worldcat.org/

COPAC (free public access) Includes the library catalogue records from most British universities and the national libraries, with more research libraries and collections being added all the time.
http://www.copac.ac.uk/copac/

British Library (free public access)
http://www.bl.uk/

National Library of Scotland (free public access)
http://www.nls.uk/

National Library of Wales (free public access)
http://www.llgc.org.uk/

The European Library is a free service that offers access to the resources of the 48 national libraries of Europe in 20 languages. Resources can be both digital or bibliographical (books, posters, maps, sound recordings, videos, etc.). Currently The European Library gives access to 150 million entries across Europe. The amount of referenced digital collections is constantly increasing. Quality and reliability are guaranteed by the 48 collaborating national libraries of Europe. The European Library is a non-commercial organisation.
http://www.theeuropeanlibrary.org/

Oxford University's online library catalogue OLIS (free public access)
http://library.ox.ac.uk or through the interface Search Oxford Libraries Online: http://solo.ouls.ox.ac.uk (electronic resources not available outside Oxford)

Royal Historical Society Bibliography (free public access)
http://www.rhs.ac.uk/bibl/bibwel.asp
It is worth having a look at its tutorials on search techniques before starting to search this: see
http://www.rhs.ac.uk/bibl/docs/tutorials.html

History On-line from the Institute of Historical Research
http://www.history.ac.uk/search/welcome.html and also its theses section
http://www.history.ac.uk/ihr/Resources/Theses/

Historical abstracts (institutional subscription required)
http://library.dialog.com/bluesheets/html/bl0039.html for details without access

EThOS, for digital access to UK theses (from 2009)
http://www.ethos.ac.uk/

Index to Theses (institutional subscription required)
http://www.theses.com/

UMI Dissertation Services (institutional subscription required)
http://www.umi.com/products_umi/dissertations/

The Wellesley Index to Victorian periodicals, 1824-1900
(institutional subscription required). Provides access to printed
sources of Victorian thought and opinion.
http://wellesley.chadwyck.com/marketing/about.jsp

ATLA Religion (institutional subscription required)
http://www.atla.com/products/catalogs.html but free access to
ATLA Selected Religion Web Sites Project: ATSRW List of
Catalogued Web Sites
http://www.atla.com/tsig/atsrw/catalogedsiteslist.html

A publicly available site is the "Internet Guide to Religion" at the
Wabash Center
http://www.wabashcenter.wabash.edu/resources/guide_headings.aspx
It is useful to study its "Internet Guide Search Tips" before starting
your search:
http://www.wabashcenter.wabash.edu/resources/article2.aspx?id=681
7

FRANCIS (institutional subscription required, through OCLC/First
Search, Proquest-CSA or Ovid). An international, multilingual,
multidisciplinary humanities and social sciences comprehensive
bibliographic resource, containing all types of materials dating from
1984, which includes the *Baptist Quarterly*, the *American Baptist
Quarterly* and the *Caribbean Quarterly* among the journals it indexes.
Produced by the French CNRS Institute for Scientific and Technical

Information.
http://international.inist.fr/article59.html

British Humanities Index (institutional subscription required)
accessible via CSA Illumina, see
http://www.csa.com/factsheets/bhi-set-c.php

Arts & Humanities Citation Index/Social Sciences Citation Index
(institutional subscription required) accessible via ISI Web of
Knowledge/Web of Science. See:
http://www.thomsonreuters.com/products_services/scientific/Web_of_Science
http://www.thomsonreuters.com/products_services/scientific/Arts_Humanities_Citation_Index

(The search in multi-disciplinary web-based databases for reviews of
the two books by Catherine Hall[6] and Geoff Oddie[7] mentioned in
Section 5(d)(v) below provides a brilliant example of the search
techniques and alternative approaches required when looking for
material on a subject as diverse as Baptist missionary history. A
comparative search of ATLA, *Historical Abstracts,* Web of Science
(for *Arts & Humanities Citation Index* and *Social Sciences Citation
Index*) and CSA Illumina (for *British Humanities Index*, *Sociological
Abstracts* and *Worldwide Political Science abstracts*) produced the
following results. ATLA was the only one of the three databases to
list the reviews in the *Baptist Quarterly*, listed no other reviews for
Catherine Hall's *Civilising subjects*, but also listed the reviews of
Oddie's *Imagined Hinduism* in the *Journal of Religious History* and
the *International Bulletin of Missionary Research* noted in the
Bibliography below, but no others. None of these were also indexed
by either Web of Science (*Arts & Humanities Citation Index* and
Social Sciences Citation Index) or CSA Illumina (*British Humanities
Index*, *Sociological Abstracts* and *Worldwide Political Science
abstracts*). Out of the nineteen records of reviews of *Civilising
subjects* identified by *Arts & Humanities Citation Index* and *Social*

Sciences Citation Index together (and both definitely need to be
checked) only four were also identified by CSA databases, but they
located four additional reviews. For *Imagined Hinduism* CSA
retrieved only one review, via *Sociological Abstracts,* while Web of
Science retrieved six, although it was noticeable that none were
retrieved when the author of the book was included in the search in
addition to the title, just as only one of the Hall book was retrieved
under her name, as against the nineteen when searched on title alone.
The need to check both the Arts and Humanities and the Social
Sciences subject areas in both these search tools for interdisciplinary
books such as these was very apparent. Neither *Historical Abstracts*
nor the *RHS Bibliography* were of much use in finding reviews of
either book.)

Mundus http://www.mundus.ac.uk/. "The Mundus Gateway is a free
web-based guide to more than four hundred collections of overseas
missionary materials held in the United Kingdom. These materials,
comprising the archives of British missionary societies, collections of
personal papers, printed matter, photographs, other visual materials
and artefacts, are held in a large number of libraries, record offices
and other institutions in England, Northern Ireland, Scotland and
Wales. The Mundus Gateway makes it easier for researchers to locate
these collections and obtain sufficient information about their
contents to enable effective planning of research visits.

The web-guide contains a collection-level description of each
collection including valuable background information and a summary
of contents. There is a facility for freetext searches as well as searches
by personal names, organization names, place-names and subjects.
Clickable maps are supplied to assist with geographical searches. The
Mundus Gateway contains full access and location details of each
holding institution. The Links page contains links to useful web sites
in the British Isles, Continental Europe and the wider world, while the
Gallery provides a snapshot of the extensive range of visual materials
to be found in many missionary collections."[8]

Archives

The National Archives (free public access)
http://www.nationalarchives.gov.uk/

A2A – Access to Archives (free public access)
http://www.a2a.org.uk/

The National Register of Archives (free public access)
http://www.nationalarchives.gov.uk/nra/

Archon: "The ARCHON Directory includes contact details for record repositories in the United Kingdom and also for institutions elsewhere in the world which have substantial collections of manuscripts noted under the indexes to the National Register of Archives." (free public access)
http://www.nationalarchives.gov.uk/archon/

Archives Hub (free public access) A national gateway to descriptions of archives in UK universities and colleges
http://www.archiveshub.ac.uk/

National Union Catalogue of MS Collections (free public access via OCLC WorldCat to US archival records)
http://www.loc.gov/coll/nucmc/

There are links to some of these and to some other sites of potential interest, including a page of advice and guidance on "Useful Contacts for Nonconformist Archives" on the Religious Archives Group's website at http://rylibweb.web.its.manchester.ac.uk/rag2/links/

Biographical

Oxford Dictionary of National Biography (subscription required, but available in most public libraries and at home with a public library membership card number)
http://www.oxforddnb.com/

Genuki (free public access)
http://www.genuki.org.uk/

Who's Who and Who was Who (subscription required, but may be available through your local public library under the MLA "Reference Online" agreement)
http://www.ukwhoswho.com/public/home.html

KnowUK (subscription required, but may be available through your local public library under the MLA "Reference Online" agreement) Includes current information from over one hundred of the most widely used reference publications in the UK:
http://www.knowuk.co.uk/

Guides

The National Archives' Local History guides (free public access)
http://www.nationalarchives.gov.uk/localhistory/

BBC's History Trail on Local History (free public access)
http://www.bbc.co.uk/history/lj/locallj/preview.shtml

BBC's Family History pages (free public access)
http://www.bbc.co.uk/history/familyhistory/

(Reference shelves, Angus Library, Regent's Park College, Oxford RPC)

(b) Printed general sources

Most of the general printed bibliographical sources quoted in my previous paper *Sources for the study of Baptist history* [1] have now been superseded by some of the above-mentioned websites and online library catalogues, although it is always worth checking the coverage of online catalogues, which may not include a library's older holdings. A particular example is *COPAC*, on which the coverage of many university and research libraries' early and pre-20th Century holdings may as yet (2009) be only partial, despite a number of CURL (Consortium of University and Research Libraries, now Research Libraries UK) projects aimed at increasing the coverage of 19th

Century holdings. Similarly, the coverage of the English Short Title Catalogue (ESTC), at least insofar as British libraries' pre-1800 holdings is concerned, is far from complete (or accurate). Nevertheless, the ESTC should still be a first port of call for pre-1800 printed primary sources on and of English dissenting history, incorporating as it does revisions of Pollard & Redgrave's *Short-title catalogue of books printed in England, Scotland, & Ireland and of English books printed abroad 1475-1640*[9] and Wing's similar *Short-title catalogue for 1641-1700*[10], in addition to 18th century works.

An example of a useful unique library, whose online catalogue currently only contains details of all books and periodicals acquired since 1950, plus so far only a small percentage of its pre-1950 acquisitions, is the London Library, although its retrospective cataloguing project is currently adding records for all the Library's one million volumes to the online catalogue at a rate of on average 2,000 titles (3,000 volumes) each month (see http://www.londonlibrary.co.uk/collections/retrospective.htm and its latest newsletters). (A search on the subject keyword "Baptists" produced 40 titles on a varied range of topics.) For full coverage of pre-1950 acquisitions, one also needs to consult the printed catalogues[11].

A study of *local* Baptist history should begin at the local public library, particularly if there is a local studies section, and at the local County or City Record Office. While most public library catalogues are probably now available online and the holdings of County Record Offices indexed on Access2Archives (A2A), with details of the repository on Archon (see above), they are far from complete, and a visit to the local studies library or record office to consult its card catalogues and other resources may well result in additional sources being found which could not have been located online. Similarly, while most local newspapers, which can be of great use when writing your church's history, are now likely to have an online presence, it may well not go back very far and you will need to consult the microfilm, and even hard copy, back files of the newspaper to trace your church's history.

Although such general printed bibliographical guides and good old-fashioned library card catalogues are rapidly becoming obsolete, their chief limitations being that it is only possible to search for one element of a publication at a time (author's surname, first significant word in the title, proper name as subject, general subject term, for example), where you still come across them it is worth getting to know how they are arranged and spending some time browsing through them at random. One of their advantages over modern electronic catalogues is the opportunity they provide for serendipity, like wandering around open shelves in a library, when your attention can be drawn to some obscure document which you would never have found through a systematic electronic subject search.

3. Online and printed sources for dissenting history in general

(Portrait of John Bunyan in Regent's Park College, Oxford Main Library RPC)

Much of what has been said above with regard to the general principles of bibliographic searching, whether online or in printed bibliographies, is applicable here. The Library of Congress Subject Heading "Dissenters, religious – England – history" would be a useful way of searching an online library catalogue by subject, but be prepared if you just use "Dissenters, religious – England" for a large number of records to be retrieved – 714 on Oxford University's online catalogue on one occasion. Some relevant and useful titles are also likely to be available electronically in full-text for those with access to such resources as Oxford Scholarship Online and other electronic resources, as well as on many American public websites (see section 5(a) below).

A selection of useful websites in addition to those listed in sections 2(a) and 5(a) includes the following:

http://www.exlibris.org/nonconform/engdis/bibliography.html. This provides quite an extensive bibliography of printed works on the subject of English Dissenters. The introduction to this section states that "ExLibris focuses here on English dissenters prior to and during the civil war/revolution in England as well as during the Interregnum. We view the information broadly, incorporating a variety of religious and social movements and viewpoints that were active at levels of state, and among the élites and common folk."[12] Intute describes the site thus:

> "The ExLibris website provides detailed discussion on religious dissenters prior to, during, and just after the English Civil Wars and Interregnum. ... The discussion of the dissenters is divided by religious grouping (so, for example, there is a section on Baptists and a section on Muggletonians) and each area provides details on the group's aims, goals, achievements and influential leaders. There is a considerable bibliography which, although missing a few details on some publications, is of very wide scope and highly beneficial to any student or researcher in English religious, social or political history."[13]

An overview of religion in Victorian Britain, containing referenced, signed articles, is provided at http://www.victorianweb.org/religion/relov.html. Intute describes the site thus:

> "Edited by George P. Landow, and part of the much larger Victorian Web project, the Religion in Victorian Britain Web page is a useful starting point for those who wish to gain an overview of 19th century British religious denominations, trends, and writers. The site's introductory Timeline of Religion and Philosophy, and its exhaustive list of categories (organised

under headings including Denominations, Dissenters, and the Bible, Interpretation, and Religious Symbolism) offer sound introductory material for an undergraduate audience. There is a helpful bibliography, but unfortunately the accompanying list of links to primary literature has not been updated recently, and so includes a high proportion of broken links. Written by graduate students and scholars from the UK and USA, Religion in Victorian Britain is a well-designed site which may prove valuable to those teaching undergraduates in either religion or church history."[14]

The following excerpt from the introduction to its extensive section on Dissenters gives an indication of its flavour:

"The term Dissenter refers to a number of Protestant denominations -- Presbyterians, Baptists, Quakers, Congregationalists, and others -- which, because they refused to take the Anglican communion or to conform to the tenets of the restored Church of England in 1662, were subjected to persecution under various acts passed by the Cavalier Parliament between 1661 and 1665. ... After the Toleration Act was passed in 1689, Dissenters were permitted to hold services in licensed meeting houses and to maintain their own preachers (if they would subscribe to certain oaths) in England and Wales. But until 1828 such preachers remained subject to the Test Act, which required all civil and military officers to be communicants of the Church of England, and to take oaths of supremacy and allegiance. Though this act was aimed primarily at Roman Catholics, it nevertheless excluded Dissenters as well."[15]

The Wabash Center's "Internet Guide to Religion" links to various useful websites, including http://puritanism.online.fr/, which, while more relevant to section 5(a) below on digitized primary texts, does state that

"To understand the founders of Puritan New England, their
motives and their deeds, it is important to be familiar with the
early history of the Puritan movement back in England.
Therefore I have also included English sources regarding the
history of Puritanism and even Protestantism at the bottom of
this page. Even though it is somewhat relevant, I have not gone
as far as including sources on Lollardy. I have tried to focus on
what came to be called 'Early Modern England', a period that
coincides with the history of Puritanism since Puritanism can
be said to have started in England some time between the
Elizabethan settlement of 1559 and 1563. Discontented with
what they viewed as Elizabeth's treacherous Act, they fought an
epic battle in Parliament to have their doctrines made official,
but failed at the end of the sixteenth century. The movement
went underground and thrived until emigration became
necessary in the face of Laudian repression"[16].

Moving from the virtual world to the physical world of books,
archives and libraries, "Dr Williams's Library is the pre-eminent
research library of English Protestant nonconformity. Established
under the will of Dr Daniel Williams, the Library is one of the oldest
open to the public still conducted on its original benefaction."[17] An
important example of bibliographical source material not yet
accessible online is the catalogue of Dr Williams's Library (for
details of the library go to http://www.dwlib.co.uk/dwlib/index.html),
although there are projects planned, if the requisite funding is
forthcoming, to convert the catalogue of first the Congregational
Library, and then, if successful, that of Dr Williams's Library itself,
into a new online electronic catalogue. It does already subscribe to the
ESTC for its earlier printed material and to the National Register of
Archives for its manuscript collection. Its printed catalogues and
accessions lists[18] can be consulted in many university and large public
reference libraries. Dr Williams's Library contains far more
bibliographical reference tools than the Angus Library, so a study of
the background to dissenting history in general and Baptist history in

particular should ideally include a visit there quite early in your research. A particularly useful bibliographical tool is the "Bibliography of Early Nonconformity"[19].

A useful bibliography of guides to nonconformist source material is included appended to Clive Field's article "Preserving Zion: the anatomy of Protestant nonconformist archives in Great Britain and Ireland"[20], which, while the text is of more relevance to section 5 below on primary sources, cites some helpful guides to nonconformist records, even though some of them are by now distinctly out-of-date. For example, Michael Mullett's bibliography[21] is by now as out of date as my own previous guide[1]. Some other guides, such as those by Steel and Shorney, are mentioned in section 5(d)(i) below on printed guides to manuscript archives.

Finally, the bibliographies to some of the standard works of dissenting history, such as those by Geoffrey Nuttall[22] and Michael Watts[23] can be helpful in identifying general background works on dissenting history. Other useful titles with extensive bibliographies include Dale Johnson's *The changing shape of English nonconformity*[24], although, as the editorial review in the *Baptist Quarterly*[25] points out, the book yields less than its very general title suggests, it being **not** a general history of nonconformity in this period but an exploration of issues relating to education for the ministry in the Congregational, Baptist, Methodist and Presbyterian traditions and the resulting perceptions of ministry in connection with nonconformist identity and theology and its engagement with secular culture. An alternative review from a distinctly American perspective is provided in *Church history, 69(1)*[26]. Similarly, Kenneth Brown's *A social history of the nonconformist ministry in England and Wales, 1800-1930*[27] sets 19th century Baptist ministerial training in the wider context, while for a slightly earlier period Deryck Lovegrove's *Established church, sectarian people: itinerancy and the transformation of English dissent, 1780-1830*[28] deals with the specific topic of itinerancy and dissent and contains a very useful bibliography, particularly for Association records.

While concentrating specifically on nineteenth century controversies within the Congregationalists and the Baptists, Mark Hopkins' *Nonconformity's romantic generation: evangelical and liberal theologies in Victorian England*[29] sets these against the background of Victorian nonconformist theology and his bibliography is useful for these two strands of dissenting thought at that time. Histories of evangelicalism, such as those by David Bebbington[30] and Mark Noll[31], should not be forgotten in this context, or for the twentieth century some of the useful contributions in *Protestant nonconformity in the twentieth century*[32], edited by Alan Sell and Anthony Cross. Alan Sell himself goes into more detail in *Nonconformist theology in the twentieth century*[33], reviewed by Keith Clements in *Baptist Quarterly* 42(7).

This is just a small random selection of works on the subject containing useful bibliographies: a search of Oxford University's resources under the specific subject heading "Dissenters, religious – England – history" resulted in 104 references. It is also well worth checking for theses and dissertations on related subjects and following up their bibliographies (see 4(b)(vii) below). Similarly, Paternoster's series *Studies in Evangelical history and thought* and *Studies in Christian history and thought,* in which a number of the titles quoted above appeared, many of which originated as doctoral theses, will yield many more potentially useful titles and its series *Paternoster Theological Monographs* may also contain some relevant material.[34] (For more on Paternoster's Baptist series see below, sections 4(b)(i) and (vii).

(Logo of the Baptist Historical Society used by permission of the President)

4. Secondary sources specific to Baptist history

(a) Electronic/digital

A very brief summary of British Baptist history, or more specifically of the Baptist Union of Great Britain, for those with no knowledge of the history at all, is provided in the form of a timeline on the Baptist Union of Great Britain website at: http://www.baptist.org.uk/baptist_life/baptist_history.html . Other useful British websites include those of the Baptist Historical Society http://www.baptisthistory.org.uk and the Strict Baptist Historical Society http://www.strictbaptisthistory.org.uk (whose library catalogue is now searchable online). The website of the Baptist Union of Wales at http://www.buw.org.uk/ has little of a historical nature within it, although it is advertising Michael Collis' book on Shropshire Baptist history on its News page in March 2009. On the other hand, the website of the Baptist Union of Scotland at http://www.scottishbaptist.org.uk/ has quite an extensive summary history of Baptists in Scotland at http://www.scottishbaptist.org.uk/history.htm. The Association of Baptist Churches in Ireland (Northern Region) carries details of the Society and some historical material on its website at http://www.baptistsinireland.org/ , while the Southern Region of the Association, working in the Republic of Ireland, has a little historical material on its website at http://www.baptistireland.org/ . Even some

of the Oxford University Press titles available on Oxford Reference
Online through many local public libraries, such as the *Concise
Oxford Dictionary of the Christian Church*[35], the *Oxford Companion
to British History*[36] and the *Dictionary of British History*[37], can give
you some useful brief notes.

The Baptist World Alliance Heritage and Identity Commission
http://www.bwa-baptist-heritage.org/ provides some useful links,
listing Baptist heritage websites on http://www.bwa-baptist-
heritage.org/web-her.htm, although some of these are not always up-
to-date. From the USA the Baptist History and Heritage Society
http://www.baptisthistory.org/, the American Baptist Historical
Society http://www.abhsarchives.org/ and the Southern Baptist
Historical Library and Archives http://www.sbhla.org/ also have lists
of and links to other useful Baptist historical websites (the majority
American), some more up-to-date than others.

http://www.baptistheritage.com is a site which comes from none of
these on its own, but under "Who are we?" explains "The
baptistheritage.com Council was initiated as part of a larger agenda of
the District of Columbia Baptist Convention, 'to promote harmony of
feeling and concert of action on the part of all Baptists throughout the
Nation.' More specifically the council was formed to develop a
website to provide resources for study of Baptist history, principles,
and traditions, primarily in North America."[38] This is a particularly
useful site for online Baptist historical resources, especially E.C.
Starr's *A Baptist bibliography* (see 4(b)(i) below for details of the
print publication). Now that this is available online, although not yet
fully searchable in its entirety, at
http://www.baptistheritage.com/resources/starr.htm it is possible also
to access a good proportion of the references in W.T. Whitley's *A
Baptist bibliography, 1526-1837* (see 4(b)(i) below for details of the
print publication), but since the online version of Starr has been
scanned from the printed edition, the limitations and inaccuracies of
the original printed work (see below) still apply. It is nonetheless an

extremely useful resource for the study of Baptist history and many of the outdated location references can nowadays be corrected by accessing WorldCat, ESTC or COPAC.

This section should perhaps have begun with the salutary reminder provided at the start of The Baptist Observer's "Baptist history online resources: books and websites" page at http://www.yellowstone.net/baptist/history.htm:

> "Those who would research Baptist history via the Internet be warned: there is an abundance of information about Baptist history, but most of it comes from biased perspectives which are fed from personal agendas.
>
> There is a long-held saying among Baptists: when you get two Baptists together, you get three different opinions! This is most evident when one reads online Baptist history resources: many seem bent on proving that their particular view of Baptist history is the one and only true understanding of Baptist history.
>
> History, in fact, is subject to various (and often contradictory) interpretations. Baptist history is not exempt from the interpretive confusion. Indeed, Baptists are even in disagreement over how they originated!"[39]

This site provides links to Baptist history websites and a selection of original Baptist sources available online. It lists the following:

"Baptist History Websites: An Expanded Listing

The links below are for informational purposes, serving to provide a sampling of the material available online.

___

A Brief History of Baptists -- a short summary of Landmarkist history
beliefs

A Primer on Baptist History -- generally a good early history
summary, but with a Reformed agenda

American Baptist Historical Society -- the official website

BaptistHeritage.Com -- from the Baylor University Baptist Studies
Department

Baptist Historical Society (UK) -- the official website

Baptist History and Heritage Society -- pamphlets, books and more

BWA Heritage and Identity Commission -- from the Baptist World
Alliance

Center for Baptist Heritage and Studies -- from the Baptist General
Convention of Virginia

Center for Baptist Studies at Mercer -- publications, resources,
conferences and more

Documenting the American South -- excellent collection of primary
documents (search for "Baptist")

First London Confessions of Faith -- text of early Baptist confessions
with annotations

Founder's Journal -- devoted to the Calvinistic dimension of Baptist
history

General Baptist Net -- a great collection of primary Baptist materials

Independent, Fundamentalist Baptist History -- a brief survey

Primitive Baptist Web Station -- contains text of doctrinal abstracts
and creeds of faith

Southern Baptist Historical Library and Archives -- under the
direction of the SBC seminary presidents

Strict Baptist Historical Society -- British Baptist resources

Texas Baptist Historical Collection -- important Baptist resources
from the largest Baptist convention

The Triumph of the Southern Baptists -- a brief history of Southern
Baptists

Three Witnesses for the Baptists -- a summary of Landmarkist views
of Baptist history"[40]

A summary of early Baptist history and useful bibliography of (printed) sources can be found at http://www.exlibris.org/nonconform/engdis/baptists.html . It is, however, probably worth checking its section on the so-called Kiffin and Gould manuscripts against the footnotes in Larry Kreitzer's chapter 10[41] of *Recycling the past or researching history* mentioned in section 5(d)(v) below. The site also provides some links to a few other sites of possible interest. There are also personal websites of interest for local Baptist history: one example is Graham Ward's site relating to nonconformists and Baptists in particular in Northamptonshire at www.edintone.com which contains a wealth of useful information and links based on Northamptonshire, but with relevance further afield. Such sites can probably be located via local family history societies or regional Baptist association links (Graham Ward's site was located from the Central Baptist Association's website at http://www.centralba.org.uk/links.shtml).

A useful list of Baptist websites, albeit also largely American, can be found from the already mentioned Wabash Center's "Internet Guide to Religion", which lists Baptist sites at http://www.wabashcenter.wabash.edu/resources/result_browse.aspx?topic=657&pid=650. Another helpful American site comes from Southwestern Seminary's http://www.baptisttheology.org/ and yet anotherfrom Mercer University's Center for Baptist Studies at http://www.centerforbaptiststudies.org/ . It is currently (2009) providing information and educational resources for the observance of the 400th anniversary of Baptists at http://www.centerforbaptiststudies.org/400years/ .

When accessing any of these websites it is worth bearing in mind Intute's advice on its Virtual Training Suite tutorial on the Internet for Religious Studies http://www.vts.intute.ac.uk/he/tutorial/history/?sid=2197250&itemid=12079 :

Who?, Where? And When?

"Ask yourself:

- Who has written the information?
- Who has published it?
- Are they a trustworthy source of information?
- Are they trying to persuade me / sell me something / inform or misinform me?
- Which country is the information coming from?
- Where is it held?
- Does the origin affect the slant of the information?
- When was the information originally produced?
- Is it still useful?
- Has it been updated?
- Is it going to be updated?
- Is it being preserved in its original form?"

Each section follows these questions with advice on useful evidence which can give you clues to help answer them.

A number of other sites providing digital versions of original texts are mentioned below in section 5(a).

Finally, many classic works of Baptist history have also been digitized by Baptist Standard Bearer Inc. onto a CD-Rom, which is available for purchase online. Full details and means of purchase can be found on http://www.standardbearer.org/shop/Detail.aspx?ID=566 and
http://www.online-bible.com/baptisthistory.html .

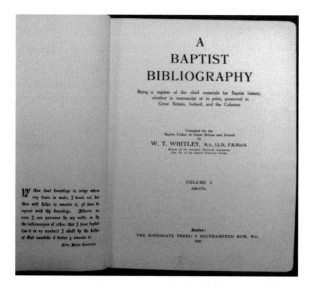

(Title page of Whitley, W.T. *A Baptist bibliography,* RPC*)*

(b) Printed

(i) Bibliographies

The printed editions of W.T. Whitley's *A Baptist bibliography, 1526-1837*[42] and E.C. Starr's *A Baptist bibliography*[43] are arranged chronologically and alphabetically (by author) respectively. Starr takes over Whitley's reference numbers for the items copied from his bibliography. Before first using Whitley's *Bibliography* it is worth spending some time learning how it is arranged and the meaning of his reference numbers. Each item is listed according to the year in which it was published and the last three digits of the reference number after the hyphen represent that year without the initial number 1. The number before the hyphen merely represents the position of the item in the sequence for that year. For example, Thomas Crosby's 4 volume *The History of the English Baptists* (see section 4(b)(ii) below), published 1738-1740, has the Whitley number 4-738, which means that in Whitley's bibliography it is the fourth item listed under the year 1738. The reference numbers for the various works by any one author can be found from the author index at the back, but if you have no idea of the date of a specific work for which you are searching and the author was a prolific writer it can take quite a long time to find it compared with online searching of ESTC or library catalogues, or even Starr's bibliography by author (although Starr can be more difficult for anonymous works). The library locations where Whitley had found the items are then indicated by capital letter codes, listed in the introduction to vol. 1 of Whitley and at the back of the first volume of Starr. For example, **A** indicates the Angus Library and **M** the British Museum Library, now the British Library. Several of the other locations are also now in the Angus Library, for example **U**, the Baptist Union Library, **H**, the Baptist Historical Society Library, **G**, the Gould collection and some of **N,** the Midland College library, Nottingham. Since Whitley's published volumes terminate at the year 1837, Starr is particularly useful for subsequent years, but the Angus Library does possess Whitley's index cards for the projected third volume of his bibliography, for works published between 1838 and 1939, which could usefully be digitised one day, despite the illegibility of some of the handwriting and confusion with regard to the sources quoted. As well as taking over Whitley's British library codes, Starr is particularly strong on North American library locations, the codes for which are listed in the first volume, but for an explanation of the codes relating to works in the American Baptist Historical Society's collections see http://abhsarchives.org/links.shtml. One limitation of Starr is that he took Whitley's entries, locations and reference numbers without verification or correction. Another is the number of entries taken from W.E. McIntyre's *Baptist authors: a manual of bibliography, 1500-1914*[44], both because the work was never completed beyond the letter D and because many of the documents listed were cited from review and advertisement notices in periodicals such as the *Baptist magazine* and locations for them have never been found.

There are a number of printed bibliographies on specific topics, such as that on *Baptists in Canada*[45], Dr Williams's Library's *Nonconformist congregations in Great Britain*[46], Athol Gill's *Bibliography of Baptist writings on baptism*[47] and D.P. Kingdon's *Bibliography of books on Baptist history*[48]. It is worth noting that a subject search of COPAC, for example, using the free text words "Baptist bibliography" and the subject keywords "Baptists" and "Bibliography" yields 123 results, because all works about Baptists, or with the word Baptist in the subject line, and where the inclusion of a bibliography or bibliographical footnotes has been noted in the record, have been included. A search of the RHS bibliography, however, using the free text keywords "Baptist history bibliography" resulted in only 11 records, five of which refer to articles in the *Baptist Quarterly*.

For further bibliographical references it is always useful to consult the bibliographies in published Baptist histories, whether general in nature, or on specific topics, churches, Associations, or individuals, whether published in book form or in periodical articles, and in unpublished academic theses and dissertations. Each of these categories will be considered in turn. Particularly useful are the titles published in Paternoster's series *Studies in Baptist history and thought* (see http://www.authenticmedia.co.uk/AuthenticSite/Authentic/theology monographs studies%20in%20baptist%20history%20and%20thought /page/2), plus some other Paternoster titles not published in this series (see section 3 above), since many of these titles were originally written as doctoral theses and therefore include extensive bibliographies. One example is Peter Shepherd's *The making of a modern denomination*[49], which has a particularly useful bibliography of primary and secondary sources for late nineteenth and early twentieth-century Baptist history.

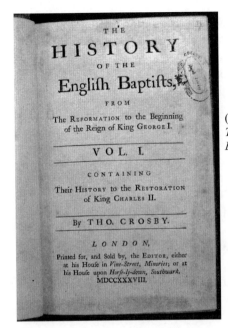

(Title page of Crosby, T.
*The history of the English
Baptists,* RPC)

(ii) Histories

For those without a basic knowledge of Baptist history a quick outline
of British Baptist history can be found in the annual *Baptist Union
Directory*[50]. As for published histories of British or English Baptists
in general a good start would be the second edition of Roger
Hayden's excellent *English Baptist history and heritage*[51], which
includes a useful brief bibliography for those commencing a study of
Baptist history and a preface not only noting reasons for studying
denominational history but also outlining many of the published
volumes mentioned here. Next, the four volumes of the Baptist
Historical Society's series *A history of the English Baptists*[52] [53] [54] [55]
will fill out this English Baptist history with further details. Appendix
II to B.R. White's first volume of these (in the revised 1996 edition)
includes a useful summary of earlier published histories by Crosby[56],

Rippon[57], Ivimey[58] (an updated index to which was compiled by
K.W.H. Howard[59]), Taylor[60], Whitley[61], Underwood[62] and Payne (for
a selection of his historical works see[63] [64] [65] [66] [67]). The following is a
selective quotation from this Appendix, but newcomers to these
works are recommended to read the whole Appendix, as well as the
Introduction, which justifies the study of specifically Baptist history
in itself.

> "From the first, Baptist historians in England have not merely
> tried to give as adequate a narrative as their sources allow but
> have seen their task as that of defending their co-religionists
> and of influencing denominational policy.
>
> This can be seen even in the work of Thomas Crosby ... *The
> History of the English Baptists* ... Apart from attempting a
> narrative history Crosby sought to put the Baptist case from
> three particular points of view ... Since Crosby's work is
> neither systematic nor analytical it is important to note that it is
> largely based on manuscripts and printed works which are still
> available to the historian.
>
> Joseph Ivimey (1773-1834) ... made the next major narrative
> contribution with his *History of the English Baptists* ... Like
> Crosby, Ivimey too set out to act both as the apologist for the
> Baptists and as their critic as well as their historian ... Since
> Ivimey's volumes were published with intervals of several
> years between each one and the next it was not surprising that
> changing concerns were reflected in them as the work
> developed ...
>
> The only General Baptist among the early historians was Adam
> Taylor (1768-1833) who produced his two-volume *A History of
> the English General Baptists* in 1818 ... Taylor ... wrote quite
> deliberately to explain the position and to describe the origins
> of his people. In his second volume Taylor dealt largely with

the history of those older congregations which had united with the new body [i.e. the General Baptists of the New Connexion] and its leaders.

During the remainder of the nineteenth century other Baptists were to produce histories of the denomination which took the story beyond the chronological limits of the classic writers already mentioned. Nevertheless, usually the later nineteenth century authors added little to the information about the seventeenth and eighteenth centuries provided by Crosby, Rippon, Ivimey and Taylor ... It was not ... until W.T. Whitley (1861-1947) that English Baptist history began to be studied in any systematic way and by modern methods ... The most recent comprehensive study, by A.C. Underwood, *The history of the English Baptists* (1947) benefited greatly from Whitley's work and provided a readable replacement for his *History*. It is significant that, consciously or unconsciously, Underwood, like his predecessors, also hoped to tell a plain tale plainly, together with a defence and explanation of the Baptist case and an attempt to mould the thinking, perhaps the policy, of the denomination.

During the last thirty years (B.R. White's book was first published in 1983) the writings of Dr E.A. Payne have pointed the way for a younger generation of Baptist historians."[68]

Among other older Baptist histories not mentioned in this summary are J.H. Wood's *A condensed history of the General Baptists of the New Connexion*[69], J.M. Cramp's *Baptist history from the foundation of the Christian church to the close of the eighteenth century*[70] (which has a revised title for a later edition introduced by Joseph Angus), and Benjamin Evans' *The early English Baptists*[71], in the preface to which the author, well over a hundred years before Dr White, criticises the works of Crosby, Ivimey, Adam Taylor and J.H. Wood, and congratulates Underhill for the Hanserd Knollys Society's publications (see section 5.b below). He summarizes Baptist history to date (1862) thus: "Rippon's Registers, the Magazines, Histories of Associations, Circular Letters, &c, supply epitomes, &c. Other writers have not done us justice. The complaint has been uttered again and again. Crosby complained of Neal; Ivimey is equally loud against Messrs. Bogue and Bennett" and states that his aim "has been to present to the minds of my readers as graphic a sketch of the illustrious founders of our body as possible"[72]. Evans' work is however written in the successionist mode, and does not first mention the early Baptists Smyth and Helwys until chapter six of the first volume[73], earlier chapters dealing with the Lollards and the reigns of Henry II, Henry VII, Henry VIII, Edward VI, Mary and Elizabeth.

J.C. Carlile's *The story of the English Baptists*[74], which does contain a bibliography and index and some illustrations of a few significant figures in Baptist history, in 1905 brings the story to the dawn of the twentieth century. How far his picture of the "new outlook" was fulfilled can perhaps be judged by the later volumes mentioned above, in particular Ian Randall's *The English Baptists of the twentieth century*[55] published exactly a century later.

Histories of Baptists in the British Isles outside England are not covered in depth here but for Scotland include George Yuille's *History of the Baptists in Scotland from pre-Reformation times*[75] (1926) and *The Baptists in Scotland*[76] edited by David Bebbington (1988), both published by the Baptist Union of Scotland. The latter volume, written by different contributors, contains bibliographical footnotes to each chapter which provide further useful sources of Scottish Baptist history, while the bibliography of Brian Talbot's *The search for a common identity: the origins of the Baptist Union of Scotland 1800-1870*[77] and the bibliographical websites and catalogues noted above can direct you to more recent works: the Library of Congress subject heading "Baptists – Scotland – history" is the most useful for this. The short work by John Fisher published by the Scottish Baptist History Project, *Impelled by faith: a short history of the Baptists in Scotland*[78], provides in forty-four pages a very useful background summary.

For Wales T.M. Bassett's *The Welsh Baptists*[79] is the most comprehensive in English, with a more specifically missionary orientation in his *The Baptists of Wales and the Baptist Missionary Society*[80], while an earlier period of Welsh Baptist history is covered in Densil Morgan's Oxford D.Phil. thesis *The development of the Baptist movement in Wales between 1714 and 1815 with particular reference to the evangelical revival*[81]. The earliest Welsh Baptist historian, in both Welsh and English, was Joshua Thomas, minister at Leominster Baptist Church (his manuscript history of which is in the Angus Library), whose *A history of the Baptist Association in Wales, from the year 1650, to the year 1790*[82] and *Hanes y Bedyddwyr, ymhlith y Cymr,*[83] were foundational and heavily used by John Rippon in the Baptist Annual Register [244]: his *History of the Welsh Association* was published by Rippon as a supplement to the *Register*. Ken Manley quotes Rippon's reference to "the indefatigable pursuits of Mr. Thomas of Leominster, a minister this, probably not inferior to any of his contemporaries in an historical acquaintance with the English Baptists, and who is thought to be the best informed person on earth, concerning the origin and progress of the present baptized churches in Wales"[84]. This should serve as a reminder that many of the sources for Welsh Baptist history, both primary and secondary, are in Welsh and those without Welsh should proceed with caution, even though few are quoted here. This even applies to students of English Baptist history, on account of the number of Welsh preachers who crossed the border into England and had a profound effect on English Baptist history. Later histories in Welsh of Welsh Baptists include J. Spinther James[85] and Thomas Shankland[86].

Baptists in Ireland have been handled by Joshua Thompson, in his Oxford D.Phil. thesis *Baptists in Ireland, 1792-1922: a dimension of Protestant dissent*[87] and his shorter history of the Baptist Union of Ireland, *Century of grace*[88]. Articles in the *Irish Baptist Historical*

Society Journal[89], also edited by Joshua Thompson, are another useful source of material relating to Irish Baptist history.

I will not discuss Strict Baptist sources in great detail, but Kenneth Dix's excellent book *Strict and Particular*[90] provides a comprehensive history of Strict Baptists, while the Strict Baptist Historical Society's earlier series *The Strict Baptist chapels of England*[91] and S.F. Paul's *Further history of the Gospel Standard Baptists*[92] have useful information about Strict Baptist chapels. Other more specific works from a particular (in either sense of the word) standpoint, and covering a limited period of Baptist history, but each with extensive and useful bibliographies, include Peter Naylor's *Calvinism, Communion and the Baptists: a study of English Calvinistic Baptists from the late 1600s to the early 1800s*[93] or his earlier *Picking up a pin for the Lord*[94], Robert Oliver's *History of the English Calvinistic Baptists*[95], which includes an extensive bibliography of primary and secondary sources and a useful summary of Strict Baptist magazines, and R. Philip Roberts' *Continuity and change: London Calvinistic Baptists and the Evangelical Revival, 1760-1820*[96].

Another work dealing with a specific period of Baptist history, but from a novel standpoint, is Stephen Wright's *The early English Baptists, 1603-1649*[97], reviewed by Stephen Copson in the *Baptist Quarterly* vol. 41, no. 6. The reviewer states that while Dr Wright challenges the neat division of the consensus of Baptist history on the seventeenth century origins of the General and Particular Baptists, he draws on a wealth of primary sources in church and legal records, providing a significant contribution to our understanding about how Baptists developed in the 1640s and why they belonged to differing factions, bringing "a fresh approach to familiar material". He concludes that the book is a "welcome breath of fresh air blowing over the embers" and that "whether we agree with all the findings or not, for anyone seriously interested in looking at Baptist beginnings in seventeenth-century England, Dr Wright sets down a challenge which cannot be ignored"[98]. Two further modern works also limited to seventeenth-century Baptists are Mark Bell's *Apocalypse how?: Baptist movements during the English Revolution*[99] and David Copeland's *Benjamin Keach and the development of Baptist traditions in seventeenth-century England*[100], both of which contain useful bibliographies.

The lack of objectivity noted above in many of the Baptist histories of the past continues today, particularly in Baptist histories originating in North America, which, while including some background on the British scene, often leave significant gaps in their treatment of British Baptist origins and in their bibliographical citations. However, they can be very useful for the study of Baptist history worldwide and in particular in North America. This applies to Robert G. Torbet's *A history of the Baptists*, first published by Judson Press in 1950, but with a British edition published by Carey Kingsgate Press in 1966 and later revised American editions[101]. Although the first part describes "Baptist beginnings", with an introductory chapter on "An approach to Baptist history", and part two treats "British and European Baptists", by far the greater part of the book (pages 201-503 in the British edition) deals with "American Baptists". However, the work has some useful appendices, including an international chronological table from 1525 to 1965 and an extensive bibliography of largely nineteenth and early twentieth-century material, predominantly but not exclusively American in origin, with some German titles included for Anabaptist history.

More modern examples of American Baptist histories include the works of W.G. McLoughlin[102] and [103], Leon Mc Beth[104] (for his companion *Sourcebook* [355] see below), William H. Brackney[105] [106] [107] [108] [109], Bill Leonard[110] [111], P.R. and K.E. Durso[112], Jerry Sutton[113], A.W. Wardin's *The twelve Baptist tribes in the United States*[114], and a new title, James Leo Garrett's *Baptist theology: a four-century study*[115]. These are all useful sources for an overview of Baptist history, and their bibliographies repay study, even while those

supposedly also recounting British Baptist history sometimes omit
some significant British works. It is a good idea to read reviews of
such works in the *Baptist Quarterly* where available, as well as in the
American Baptist Quarterly and *Baptist History and Heritage*, for an
idea of what in the British literature may have been left out of the
bibliographies of such American works. An example is Brackney's *A
genetic history of Baptist thought*, reviewed in BQ[116], BH&H[117] and
ABQ[118]. A useful comparative editorial review of three of the
histories of American Baptists mentioned above can be found in the
Baptist Quarterly for October 2006[119], in which the editor outlines the
different emphases of each (thematic, chronological and
chronological/analytical) and stresses that "each volume brings its
own special interests so the serious scholar and college libraries really
need all three"[120]. Some such reviews can be located via ATLA[121] and
if you have access to a university with a subscription to the full text
ATLAS[122] you may even be able to find the text of the review online
(though not when it is in the *Baptist Quarterly*), or via Arts &
Humanities Citation Index[123] or British Humanities Index[124], if you
have access to a library or university with subscriptions to these via
Web of Knowledge/Web of Science. It is always worth checking the
periodicals included in such online services, as significant ones from
the Baptist historical point of view (such as the *Baptist Quarterly*)
may not have been included, or if they have, like the RHS
Bibliography at http://www.rhs.ac.uk/bibl/bibwel.asp, may only
include articles and not reviews. It is perhaps worth pointing out that
the Baptist Historical Society's website at
http://www.baptisthistory.org.uk includes the contents of each issue,
including reviews, from volume 38, No. 5 (January 2000) onwards.

Until fairly recently published Baptist historical material about parts
of the world other than the British Isles and North America, at least in
book form, has been relatively limited, but this is gradually being
rectified, particularly with regard to European Baptists, thanks to the
publications of the International Baptist Theological Seminary, for
example[125] [126] [127] [128]. Current research projects in this area at IBTS can

be viewed at http://www.ibts.eu/research/ibas and see also the related publications in the Paternoster series *Studies in Baptist history and thought*[129] [130] [131] [132], the last three of which, *The Gospel in the world, Baptist identities* and *Baptists and mission*, consist of papers from the first, third and fourth International Conferences on Baptist Studies respectively. (These conferences have been held every three years since 1997 in different countries and even continents and provide a wealth of scholarly research into Baptist history and thought.) The *Baptist Quarterly* has also included articles about the history of Baptists in other countries, such as Ghana[133], Bulgaria[134], Estonia[135] [136], Poland[137], Romania[138], and the Netherlands[139].

The original classic work on European Baptists was J.H. Rushbrooke's *The Baptist movement in the continent of Europe*, first published in 1915 and revised in 1923[140], which in two hundred brief pages outlines the history of Baptists in twenty-two different European countries divided into five regions, commencing with an account of the German pioneer Johann Gerhard Oncken and in the revised edition ending with an account of the London conference of 1920. Bernard Green's works on Rushbrooke[141] himself and the European Baptist Federation[142] take the story of Baptist cooperation in Europe through the twentieth century, while his (forthcoming) 2009 work on *European Baptists and the Third Reich*[143] focuses on a specific aspect and era of that European Baptist history. A selection of modern works on Baptists in specific European countries can be found at[144] [145] [146] [147] [148]. Reviews of some of these can be located via ATLA, for example Heather Coleman's *Russian Baptists and spiritual revolution,* which was reviewed in an editorial review article in the *Baptist Quarterly vol. 41, no. 6*[149], where the Editor points out that this is "a very fine study, written from the perspective of social-science modernization theory, which deliberately eschews confessional apologetic"[150]. He states that the "strength of the volume lies in the range of sources consulted which extend from government files to records of the Orthodox Church, which register both their alarm at the growth of the Baptist movement and their strategies for dealing with this, to denominational records including especially the periodicals"[151]. Other works relating to European Baptists are to be published in 2009, by Ian Randall[152] and Keith Jones, as well as that by Bernard Green mentioned above. It is also worth noting the periodical *Journal of European Baptist Studies* in this context, both for its relevant articles and for its book reviews (see section 4(b)(v) below).

For the rest of the world a very brief background history with occasional bibliographic references can be found in Wardin's *Baptists around the world: a comprehensive handbook[153]*, while the official reports of the Baptist World Congresses[154] and the centenary history of the Baptist World Alliance *Baptists together in Christ, 1905-2005[155]*, with chapters describing different eras in the life of the BWA written by different historians, sets the worldwide Baptist scene, at least from the start of the twentieth century, and completes the more limited picture given by Townley Lord's earlier jubilee history of the BWA[156].

A random selection of histories of Baptists in a few specific countries includes the centenary histories of the Baptist Union of South Africa[157], the Baptist churches in Nigeria[158], and the Baptist Union of New Zealand[159] and the more recent *Baptists in colonial New Zealand* [160]edited by Martin Sutherland, and Ken Manley's history of Australian Baptists, *From Woolloomooloo to 'eternity'[161]*.

To conclude this section mention should perhaps be made of two of the many volumes of varied and useful essays relating to Baptist history in many of its guises: *Pilgrim pathways[162]* and *Recycling the past or researching history[163]*. The first of these is a Festschrift in honour of B.R. White, and contains an interesting collection of essays by historians and scholars from both sides of the Atlantic, grouped into sections entitled "Issues of Baptist identity", "The Baptist way of being the Church", "History as biography" and "Crossing boundaries". The second, published on the occasion of the 2005

Centennial Celebration of the Baptist World Alliance in Birmingham, England "is written with an eye to a global Baptist readership, as much as for scholarly consumption" and while representing high standards of academic scholarship the essays "are nevertheless accessible and thoroughly engaging for non-specialists interested in a thoughtful dialogue with the past about issues that affect Baptist identity today", according to the Foreword by Stephen Brachlow[164]. The essays cover a very wide range of topics and are written by scholars of different outlooks from both sides of the Atlantic, plus one from Latvia. They all include detailed bibliographical footnotes.

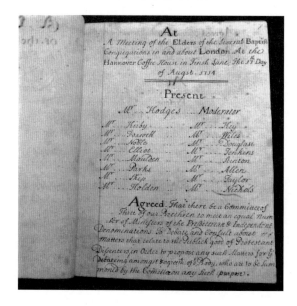

(First page of minutes of General Baptist ministers in London, 17 August 1714, RPC)

(iii) Association and regional histories

The published histories of many of the regional and local Baptist Associations provide a rich source of Baptist historical information, albeit rather variable in quality and by now in many cases in need of updating. The Appendix provides some guidelines for locating them, but the following are some worth noting.

Frank Buffard's *Kent and Sussex Baptist Associations*[165] provides a very clear and accessible guide to the different Particular and General Baptist Associations in Kent and Sussex during various eras, but especially during the 18th and 19th centuries. The complications engendered at that time by the General Baptist Assembly (to which many old General Baptist churches which did not join the New Connexion but which tended to veer towards Unitarianism belonged), the New Connexion of General Baptists, the Particular Baptists and the different strands of Strict Baptists are clarified and lists are provided of the member churches of the different General and Particular Baptist Associations, with references and a bibliography.

Thornton Elwyn's history of the Northamptonshire Baptist Association[166] provides a straightforward narrative history, with a special emphasis on some dominant personalities (particularly useful for laymen whose details are not as easily accessible as those of ministers), with lists of the Association's secretaries, treasurers, moderators, presidents and circular letters and their writers. Although its bibliography is fairly limited it includes a useful list of local church histories, not always easily obtainable elsewhere. A short and fairly limited history of the London Baptist Association was published in 1965[167], while the 250th anniversary history of the Midland (West Midland) Association[168] and F.M.W. Harrison's history of the East Midlands Association[169] provide helpful background material for those associations. However, sometimes a history of the Baptists in one part of an Association's area, such as A.S. Langley's *Birmingham Baptists, past and present*[170], can be of more use for the history of the churches in that district than the Association history. Shorter histories of individual Baptist Associations have been published in the *Baptist Quarterly* and can be located through its indexes.

Useful accounts of the Baptists in specific counties include: A.J. Klaiber's *The story of the Suffolk Baptists*[171], which mentions both Baptist Union and Strict Baptist churches and contains a detailed list of sources despite its date (1931) and an index; E.A. Payne's *The Baptists of Berkshire*[172], which is mainly a history of the Abingdon and Berkshire Associations, but also contains details of the churches and includes bibliographical footnotes, a selected bibliography and an index; and Doris Witard's *Bibles in barrels: a history of Essex Baptists*[173]. An older volume, which one would not expect from its title to be as useful as it is, is John Browne's *History of*

Congregationalism and memorials of the churches in Norfolk and Suffolk[174], which also contains sections on the Baptist churches in Norfolk and Suffolk, with separate indexes to the names of the churches and to the Baptist pastors. Much more recent county-wide Baptist histories include Stephen Greasley's *The Baptists of Derbyshire 1650-1914*[175] and Michael Collis' *Shropshire Baptist history*[176].

Of particular usefulness for reference purposes are the regional histories *Baptists of North-west England*[177] and *The Baptists of Yorkshire*[178], originally published separately, but in 1913 reprinted for the Baptist Historical Society in a new augmented edition[179]. The detailed indexes of places and people, especially in the first of these, compiled by the Baptist historian W.T. Whitley, make them a fount of information about the divisions and amalgamations of the Baptist churches in these areas and about the personalities of the ministers, although as so often with Whitley's works, the sources of his information are not always clear enough for modern historians intent on checking his data.

For the Northern Association Stephen Copson's *Association life of the Particular Baptists of Northern England, 1699-1732*[180] provides a very detailed account of the origins of the churches in that area and of the early days of that Association, in addition to providing a transcript of the association meetings between those dates, compiled from various manuscript source documents. Further useful regional histories for northern Baptists include the classic from 1846 by David Douglas[181], still of interest today despite more recent works on the Baptists of north east England, such as that by David Neil[182], which unfortunately also contains no index or bibliography, its introduction simply quoting four primary sources: Douglas' work and the Northern Baptist Association minutes in the Tyne and Wear Archives in Newcastle. Douglas, although useful, contains no index, only a rather detailed list of the contents, from which one can locate details of Thomas Tillam, David Fernie, Richard Pengilly, Joseph Angus and the churches at Newcastle, Tottlebank, Hexham, Hamsterly and Bridlington, to name but a few.

For the south west Jerom Murch's *A history of the Presbyterian and General Baptist churches in the West of England : with memoirs of some of their pastors*[183] of 1835 can still provide some interesting accounts of congregations and their ministers, arranged according to the counties of Gloucestershire, Wiltshire, Somerset, Dorset, Devon and Cornwall, and it does contain an index and some footnotes. Doel's *Twenty golden candlesticks: or a history of Baptist nonconformity in western Wiltshire*[184] was reprinted by Wiltshire County Council and the Wiltshire Family History Society in 2005 to mark the 350th anniversary of the Southwick church. John Briggs remarked in his review of this reprint in the *Baptist Quarterly*[185], that it was unfortunate that the opportunity had not been taken to bring the story up-to-date or provide any critical assessment, but this has now been rectified by the publication of Andrew D. Jones *Twenty golden candlesticks revisited*[186], also reviewed by John Briggs in the *Baptist Quarterly*[187]. The reprint of the earlier work is nevertheless of value to family historians, he asserts, in its lists of names and to wider Baptist historiography in its story of persecution, church-planting, theological controversy and schism, which often extended the church more than mission strategy did and it is also useful for its careful transcript of the local Southwick Baptist Church records.

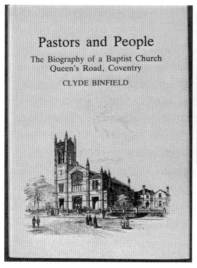

(*Left:* Cover of Binfield, C. *Pastors and people: the biography of a Baptist church, Queen's Road Coventry,* RPC/Binfield. *Above:* Olney Baptist Church, BMS)

(iv) Local church histories

The published histories of local Baptist churches can vary enormously in quality and accuracy, but can nevertheless be extremely useful in providing insights into the church life of a region, as well as the character and career of a minister. The best of them include a bibliography of sources, which notes the current whereabouts of the records of the church, and an index, at the very least of personal names. Both the Angus Library and Dr Williams's Library hold a large collection of local church histories (a list of the latter was published in 1973[188], but has sadly not been updated), but a local public library or local studies centre can normally be expected to contain a good collection of such histories from its area. Since they are often locally and privately published by the church, they may not appear in national bibliographies or library catalogues, so it can be difficult to identify those that exist. This is a good reason for depositing a copy of your church history in the Angus Library as well as in a local public library, so that it can be catalogued onto online public access catalogues (OPACs) such as OLIS (Oxford Libraries

Information Service), or others included in COPAC. It is also worth noting that many published chapel histories are reviewed in the *Baptist Quarterly*: those in the most recent volumes can be identified from the indexes on the website http://www.baptisthistory.org.uk (click on *Baptist Quarterly*). Useful sources for information on many actual chapel buildings and their architectural history, with references to published histories where applicable, are the volumes on Nonconformist chapels and meeting houses compiled by Christopher Stell originally for the Royal Commission on Historical Monuments, but latterly for English Heritage[189] [190] [191] [192].

A very small selection of the more useful such histories will be mentioned here, but it is also worth noting works not written specifically as histories of an individual church but which nonetheless have considerable bearing upon the history of a church at one period of its history. One such example is Larry Kreitzer's two volume work *'Seditious Sectaryes': the Baptist Conventiclers of Oxford 1641-1691*[193], which examines, catalogues and transcribes original source documents of various kinds in extreme detail in order to sketch out "the lives of some of the early Oxford conventiclers who eventually came to identify themselves with the Baptist cause of dissent in Oxford"[194]. As Stephen Copson states in his review on the Baptist Historical Society website: "It is an object lesson for any researcher of Baptist history or biography in the desirability to consult Anglican, parish and civil sources."[195] Similarly, the 350th anniversary volume of New Road Baptist Church in Oxford[196] is not a narrative history of that church, but rather a collection of essays on topics relating to different eras of that church's life by various contributors.

Notable among local Baptist church histories is Clyde Binfield's *Pastors and people: the biography of a Baptist church, Queen's Road Coventry*[197], which at 350 pages is a scholarly history, as one would expect from such an eminent historian, including pictures, bibliographical references and index, but it is also very readable and thus one of the best examples of the genre. As the author states in the

introduction: "This chapel history is not kings and queens history. It is
not family history. It is biography. Indeed it is the most dangerous of
all biographies, for its subject is alive and well. It is the biography of
a church"[198] Another both readable and scholarly example is Faith
Bowers' history of Bloomsbury Central Baptist Church[199], which
contains careful footnotes to the sources of references and a detailed
index of names, places, organizations and subjects. Indeed, it is
particularly interesting for its treatment of subjects as well as
pastorates.

On a much smaller scale, without an index and unfortunately printed
in a visually difficult typeface, but with detailed footnotes to each
chapter and a list of sources noting those held at the Leicestershire
Record Office, is Sheila Mitchell's *Not disobedient*[200], which provides
a very useful and detailed history of the historic Leicester Baptist
churches which comprised the present day United Baptist Church.

Some chapel histories, though short, are well indexed and sourced and
have an interest for the history of the locality beyond the church,
whether for family history or for the development of the community
or its buildings. Such is Stan Cramer's *Loughborough Baptists and
the town*[201], which uses an earlier unreferenced and unindexed history
of the General Baptists of Loughborough by Joseph Brewer[202] as a
framework, and "outlines the development of Baptist witness in
Loughborough from its small beginnings in the mid 18th century to the
present day. It shows the influence of the church in the town which
over the period changed from a small agricultural market centre
serving the local countryside ..."[203] It contains some photographs and
usefully sets the history of the church against the background history
of the town. Appendices list the ministers of the different Baptist
churches in Loughborough, membership and Sunday School statistics
obtained from the *Baptist Handbook*, documents in the Church
Collection and tombstones, while notes and references provide details
of the minutes in the Leicestershire Record Office and the Local

Studies Room of Loughborough Public Library, with church
magazine and detailed bibliographical references for each chapter.
Similarly, Doreen Gibbins' *The history and development of the
Baptist churches in Middlesborough*[204] charts the history of the
various Baptist churches in Middlesborough and the divisions from
which they arose, indexing them and locating them on a map, while
also providing a brief bibliography of secondary sources and original
church records and leaflets, showing which records are kept in the
Cleveland Archives. It also includes many facsimiles and illustrations
of the churches.

Edgar Bonsall and Edwin Robertson's *The dream of an ideal city :
Westbourne Park, 1877-1977*[205] is useful for those interested in John
Clifford, for half this chronological history concerns his ministry at
Westbourne Park, although appendices list all the ministers and
church officers, as well as membership statistics and details of the
properties and accounts. The only bibliographical notes are those on
the verso of the title page giving quotations from the church magazine
and referencing the extracts from John Clifford's books published by
the church in 1973, and its index is mainly thematic, rather than to
names.

Another General Baptist history is *Deacon's dissenters raise the
cross: the history, origin & memoirs of Cross Hills Baptist Church*[206],
whose introduction states that it shows the "fascinating story of one
small Baptist church, teaming with history, set in a few square metres
of land in one tiny corner of Leicestershire"[207], providing a
background history for 1066-1795 to the area, taken from various
secondary sources, and the history of the church 1796-1996, compiled
from records and personal accounts, with pictures, maps and
facsimiles, although there are no bibliographical references nor index.
The approach is popular, but it is useful for the early General Baptist
background and for the Deacon family, although older works such as
Godfrey's *Historic memorials*[208] or Samuel Deacon's memoirs[209]
provide more detail of that history.

Michael Hambleton's short history of Abingdon Baptist Church[210], is avowedly an interim account written in haste for the church's 350th anniversary, following the many scholarly works relating chiefly to the first twenty-five years of the church, narrating the story of the succeeding 325 years taken largely from secondary sources, and providing a framework for further research towards the major history which the author hopes will one day be written and which the church deserves. He provides a brief list of references, including the records of the church which are on long term loan in the Angus Library, and in an Appendix lists the members given in the first Church Book.

Henry Spyvee's history of Colchester Baptist Church[211] is also worth noting in this category, for its preface describes the church records available at the Essex County Record Office and states that the work is aimed both at those who know the church and want a readable account of its history and at historians who are seeking accurate information, although it has no separate bibliography or list of references. On the other hand, it does contain appendices providing a graph of membership statistics, the archaeology of the Eld Lane site, a chart of the church offshoots and lists of the ministers, church secretaries and treasurers.

The most common category of local church history is that written almost entirely with the local church members, both past and present, in mind, in celebration of a significant anniversary or building achievement. Some are reasonably scholarly in approach, with footnotes, bibliography, details of the location of the church records and possibly even an index, while others are little more than anecdotal accounts of occasions during the church's past from surviving elderly members. Among the former I would include Rosie Chadwick's history of Salendine Nook Baptist Church, Huddersfield[212], which complements John Stock and his son Percy's earlier histories of that church[213] [214], and her contribution to the history of Beulah Baptist Church, Hollinwood, Oldham[215], the first part of which gives a history of the church 1891-1956 and the second, by D.W. Joynes, "some highlights and reflections" since 1956, resulting from an oral history project within the church.

The many other celebratory church histories include those of Maidstone Baptist Church[216], carefully written from the minutes of Church and Deacons' meetings and other records, of Malvern Baptist Church[217], which does include bibliographical footnotes, of Hitchin[218], which gives a chronological history of the three hundred years of the church, with an author's note listing the church documents cited, of Eythorne[219], which gives a detailed history of the church but says that it originated in the 1540s, listing twenty-six sources, but with few precise page references, and of Princes Risborough[220], which contains contributions by different authors arranged into three sections: "Our church history", "Within living memory" and "Our church today". This includes a "historic time line" for "the church, the town and England and beyond", but is a supreme example of a booklet written entirely for the church members, past and present. Finally, J.S. Fisher's *People of the Meeting House: tales of a church in Luton*[221], is not a straightforward history of the church, but consists of a series of individual biographies of people connected with the church, not just of its ministers, the sources being listed at the end of each chapter as "Authorities", with an index to subjects, places and people. It is thus of great use to those researching the history of a family connected at some time with the church.

Sometimes an earlier history, without the modern scholarly appurtenances of footnotes, bibliography and index and which may not have a great deal of independently verifiable information about the church in question, can be of significant interest for the study of the wider history of Baptists in a particular area. Such is Fereday's *The story of Falmouth Baptists: with some account of Cornish Baptist beginnings*[222], which, though short, is very important for its account of the early Baptists in Cornwall, such as John Pendarves in the seventeenth century, the Hornblowers of Chacewater in the eighteenth (much of it taken from Rippon's *Baptist Annual Register*), Opie Smith from Bath, the itinerant ministry and Joshua Rowe of Redruth. Similarly, Frederick Overend's *History of the Ebenezer Baptist Church, Bacup*[223] is particularly useful for the background to the Baptist churches in the Rossendale valley and the only published source of the Mitchell and Crosley letters, but, as befits its publication date, it does not contain bibliographical references. From the nineteenth century Nicholson's *Authentic records relating to the Christian church now meeting in George Street and Mutley Chapels, Plymouth, 1640-1870*[224] is useful for the excerpts from transcribed source material which it contains, much of which was probably destroyed with other Plymouth records during the second World War, including not only excerpts from the church records, but also from other named manuscripts. We could perhaps also include in this section Seymour Price's *Upton: the story of one hundred and fifty years, 1785-1935*[225], which is a solid two hundred page book with index, but of its time (1935), with few footnotes and no bibliography. It is nevertheless carefully researched, with some photographs of people and the church and appendices listing ministers, church treasurers and secretaries, deacons, closing services, the Boys Brigade, a typical week's activities and the terjubilee anniversary celebrations. Similarly, Eric Hayden's *A centennial history of Spurgeon's Tabernacle*[226] tells the story of the Metropolitan Tabernacle with plenty of pictures (not all the same in the American reprint as in the original) and useful notes and index. The American edition adds a supplementary chapter "Change and decay" and Appendices providing "A catalogue of Spurgeon's literary works", "Biographies of C.H. Spurgeon", and "Other interesting Spurgeon material in published form".

Finally, if you are writing your own chapel history it would be a good idea to look at the helpful tips provided by the Strict Baptist Historical Society at http://www.strictbaptisthistory.org.uk/_private/writing.htm.

(v) Periodicals

Although I have divided periodicals between this section on using them as secondary sources and that in section 5(c)(i) below where they are treated as primary source material, this is a very arbitrary distinction, because many periodicals can be used for both secondary and primary research. For example, whilst the *Baptist Quarterly* mainly contains secondary material, and therefore is cited in this section, it has always had some transcribed primary material imbedded within it. In parallel fashion whilst the *Baptist Magazine* is generally a primary source, there is some secondary material in it, though this is often so dated in its historiography that such

(Angus Library periodical shelves, RPC)

articles may also be considered primary sources, in that they are as important for the period approach to the history they demonstrate as for any historical analysis. For this reason the *Baptist Magazine* is here chiefly discussed as a primary source (apart from its lists of churches and ministers) and the *Baptist Quarterly* as a secondary source.

The chief secondary periodical sources for specifically Baptist historical research are in the UK the *Transactions of the Baptist Historical Society*[227] and its successor *The Baptist Quarterly*[228], not forgetting *Seren Gomer*[229] and the *Irish Baptist Historical Society Journal*[89]. In the USA this role is provided on the one hand by the *American Baptist Quarterly*[230] and its predecessors, *Foundations* and *The Chronicle,* and on the other by *Baptist History and Heritage*[231]. Many other periodicals, for example the *Journal of Ecclesiastical History*[232] and *Church history*[233], include articles and book reviews relating to Baptist history, which can be located by means of the bibliographical websites cited above, in particular ATLA and the Arts and Humanities Citation Index (through Web of Science).

For research on the history of missions the *International Review of Mission*[234], published by the World Council of Churches, and the *International Bulletin of Missionary Research*[235], both now available electronically, are particularly useful, the former including a regular classified "Bibliography on Mission Studies", a cumulative online version of which is to be made available on the website of Liverpool Hope University[236]. The World Council of Churches website describes the *International Review of Mission* (IRM) as "the missiological quarterly of the WCC. Whilst its focus is ecumenical missiology, it also gives a voice to other perspectives, such as those from Pentecostal and Evangelical theologians. Articles and academic papers on important mission events are presented along with book reviews and a detailed bibliography of current literature from the Centre for the Study of Christianity in the Non-Western World (Edinburgh)"[237]. The *International Bulletin of Missionary Research* includes book reviews and book notes, dissertation notices and research articles, many of which have in the past related to Baptist missions.

For histories of Baptists in many European countries, with a special emphasis on Eastern Europe, the *Journal of European Baptist Studies*[238], published by the International Baptist Theological

Seminary in Prague, is particularly useful. Articles on the history of Baptists in Hungary, Estonia, Bulgaria, Finland, Lithuania, Moldova, Poland, Macedonia and Russia have been included. The editorial to the first number by Ian Randall stated that

> "In each issue ... there will be articles by Baptist scholars. The themes to be addressed will be of particular relevance to Baptists, although it is hoped that the journal will be read by a wider public. ... Articles will cover biblical, theological, missiological and historical study that relates to Baptist life and thought."[239]

For British local church history it is worth consulting the magazines and publications of local and family history societies, to be found in most areas, which can be located through http://www.local-history.co.uk/groups/ .and http://www.ffhs.org.uk/ respectively.

The Baptist Handbook[240], now *The Baptist Union Directory*[241], and their predecessors the *Baptist Union Annual Reports*[242] from 1832 to 1844 and the *Baptist Manual*[243] from 1845 to 1859, can be used for both secondary and primary research. From the statistical tables of the denomination, the Associations, and, most importantly, of the individual churches, a wealth of historical detail can be obtained and a local church's growth or decline traced. By following up the names of the ministers given in the statistical tables through the lists of ministers and the obituaries (an index to which is now provided online on the Baptist Historical Society's website http://www.baptisthistory.org.uk) an outline history of the church can often be compiled. However, prior to the *Baptist Handbook* itself in 1861 neither the statistics of the churches nor the lists of the ministers were published annually. Earlier lists of Baptist churches, both Particular and General, and of Baptist ministers, were published in Rippon's *Baptist Annual Register*[244], published from 1790 to 1802 (the individually published issues are not in fact identical to the four bound volumes, leading to a confusion in some pagination citations), which includes information reaching well back into the 18th century. This is a marvellous resource for both primary and secondary research and will be discussed further in section 5(c)(i). It has been analysed thoroughly by Ken Manley in his Oxford D.Phil. thesis, published as *Redeeming love proclaim*[245]. In Scotland the *Scottish Baptist Yearbook*[246] (formerly *Year-book)* provides similar statistical information on churches.

In between, in the earlier years of the nineteenth century, lists of Baptist churches and their ministers were published in the *Baptist magazine*[247], which began publication in 1809, with lists of Particular Baptist churches in England and their ministers in 1811[248], 1823[249], 1827[250], 1831[251] and 1835[252], also in Wales in 1811[253] and 1831[254], with Scotland[255] too in 1831. The lists of churches are arranged by county, the counties listed alphabetically and the place names listed alphabetically within each county. The 1823 list defines the criteria for inclusion of a church and/or its minister in this manner:

"The 'Confession of Faith' adopted and published by the General Assembly, held in London, 1689, is the standard of doctrine which the Particular Baptists have always avowed: ... By the principles of this Confession, we have endeavoured to regulate the following list, not admitting any church whose minister is known to be either Arminian, Antinomian, or Anti-Trinitarian. Some few of the churches have pastors who are Paedobaptists, but it is supposed the *majority* of the *members* are Baptists. There are some respectable Baptist *ministers*, whose names do not appear, because they are not settled with Particular churches, such as ... There are other cases, probably of Baptist ministers being pastors of *Independent* churches ..."[256] It also contains the proviso "We are aware that this list is incomplete. We have included all that are recognized by the Associations in whose Circular Letters they appear: of many, we have heard only by report..."[257]

1811 and 1823 only give the place of the town or village of the church and the Pastor's name, but 1827 and 1831 also provide the date of the formation of the church and the date of the Pastor's settlement. The 1831 volume also includes alphabetical lists of Particular and General Baptist ministers in England and of Baptist missionaries[258], while the 1835 volume has one list of churches entitled "Statistical account of Evangelical Baptist churches in England", now including both Particular and General Baptist churches in one geographically arranged list, for the first time in the format later adopted in the *Baptist Handbook*, now including the number of members of each church, the average number of hearers, the Association to which the church belonged, the number of children in the Sunday schools, the village stations and the population of the town, in addition to the information on the church and its Pastor provided in earlier years. (Full details of the page references for all these lists are given in Geoffrey Breed's *My ancestors were Baptists*[259]). From 1851 until 1860, after which it was taken over by the *Baptist Handbook*, the *Baptist Magazine* included towards the end of each volume an alphabetical list of Baptist ministers in England, with Scotland also listed separately later, giving the minister's name and place of residence. These years also provide lists of the "General Body of Dissenting ministers of the three denominations residing in and about the cities of London and Westminster; with the address of each per Post, and the Year when he became a Member of the General Body, formed 1727." The names are listed under the Baptist Board, formed 1723, the Congregational Board, formed 1727 and Presbyterian members of the Body. They also list Baptist chapels in and near London, Principal Baptist Societies (both Particular and General Baptist) and Baptist colleges and educational institutions. General Societies and Paedobaptist Societies are also listed.

The *New Baptist Miscellany* for 1831 also includes a "list of Baptist churches, with the date of their commencement, the names of their ministers and the year of their settlement"[260].

The Sword and the Trowel[261] was a periodical produced by C.H.
Spurgeon from the Metropolitan Tabernacle providing a wealth of
information about his college, its students and the churches which it
supported, as well as acting as a forum for Spurgeon's own polemics,
as in the case of the Downgrade controversy, and some of his
sermons. It is still published today by the Metropolitan Tabernacle, as
Sword & Trowel (see
http://www.metropolitantabernacle.org/?page=swordtrowel).

(Baptist luminaries, BHS)

(vi) Biographical sources

First and foremost among biographical sources is the *Oxford Dictionary of National Biography* http://www.oxforddnb.com/, available online through university libraries and now also to public library members of most local public library authorities in England, both in the library and at home using their public library membership number. Many significant Baptist ministers and public figures have been included and it can be searched by subject as well as by name. The bibliography of sources under each entry is also worth pursuing for further information about the subject of inquiry.

Most online family history searchers will also start with a Google search, which may or may not result in useful material, and family historians will be familiar with the following websites and guides, along with innumerable others, both free and expensive, which can be located through them. The most useful guides to getting started with family history are those produced by the National Archives and the BBC:

http://www.nationalarchives.gov.uk/familyhistory/default.htm?homep age=fr-more

http://www.bbc.co.uk/history/familyhistory/

An independent, but also free genealogical site is Genuki: http://www.genuki.org.uk/. One of the many subscription sites which can help with genealogical searching is http://www.ancestry.co.uk/. Although largely referencing American sources http://homepages.rootsweb.ancestry.com/~baptist/archives.html can provide some helpful links.

Now that the online versions as well as the printed volumes of *Who's Who, Who was Who*, and *KnowUK* are also available to public library members through many local public library authorities, it is worth remembering that these can also help with checking details when searching for significant individuals. Online library catalogues and bibliographic databases mentioned in section 2 above should also be checked early in your search for any printed individual or family biographies, many of which may have been privately printed and therefore be quite hard to locate. If you are searching in general for Baptist biographies, rather than for a specific individual, where Library of Congress subject headings are used the heading "Baptists – Biography" or "Baptists – England [or Great Britain, or other country] – Biography" or "Baptists – Clergy – Biography" (all of which have been used indiscriminately on OLIS for cataloguing similar publications!) are suitable headings to try, although many individual biographies will be listed with these general headings in addition to collected Baptist biographies like Ronald Thomson's *Heroes of the Baptist Church*[262], J.H. Shakespeare's *Baptist and Congregational pioneers*[263] and E.A. Payne's *The first generation* [66] and *The great succession* [67]. Some Baptists may also be included under the more general "Clergy – Biography" heading. "Clergy – Biography – Dictionaries" only brings up, rather idiosyncratically, the *Concise encyclopedia of preaching*.

Although to some extent many printed biographical dictionaries have been superseded by such online resources as those mentioned above, many are still of use in tracing the more obscure of Baptist individuals. These include the *Biographical Dictionary of British Radicals in the Seventeenth Century*[264], *The Blackwell dictionary of evangelical biography: 1730-1860*[265] and the *Biographical dictionary of evangelicals*[266], all of which include plenty of Baptists, thanks to eminent Baptist scholars among the editorial boards. For the seventeenth century there is still considerable biographical detail in A.G. Matthews' *Calamy revised*[267] and *Walker revised*[268], as well as Samuel Palmer's *The Nonconformist's memorial*[269]. Joshua Toulmin's revised editions of Daniel Neal's *The History of the Puritans*[270] are similarly useful for details of the early Baptists. For the London area, there is a wealth of biographical information about Baptist ministers in Walter Wilson's *The history and antiquities of dissenting churches and meeting houses in London, Westminster and Southwark, including the lives of their ministers*[271] and the various accounts of the ministers buried in the Bunhill Fields burial ground, notably J.A. Jones *Bunhill memorials*[272] and A.W. Light's *Bunhill Fields*[273] of 1913 and 1933 (reprinted in 2003 by Tentmaker Publications). Particularly useful for the Baptists buried in Bunhill Fields is Samuel Couling's *The dead in Christ, or, The Baptists in Bunhill Fields*[274], published by the Baptist Tract Society.

The six volume *Modern English biography*[275] of Frederic Boase, originally published in limited editions between 1892 and 1921, but reprinted in 1965, may also be of use for some nineteenth century Baptist worthies, if they died between 1851 and 1900. The three supplementary volumes need to be checked separately from the first three volumes. The introduction to the second impression states that the work contains "some 30,000 short biographical sketches of persons who died between 1851-1900 who achieved any public importance whatsoever. In most cases biographies are accompanied by a note of the particular sources used in each entry so that further research can be greatly facilitated. Boase made a special study of the existence of portraits and photographs of his subjects and gives details where these can be found. He also placed a great emphasis on exact detail particularly of births and deaths, a list of published works or theatre performances, and other facts ..."[276] Boase' object, as stated in the preface to the first edition, was to cover the careers of not only well known people but also to survey the lives of other interesting people and even foreigners living in England and some nationals of British colonies. The material was gleaned from obituaries and reports published in *The Times,* the *Illustrated London News* and other journals, local newspapers, the transactions of learned societies, parish and church registers, the records of the Registrar General at Somerset House, published memoirs, the correspondence of private individuals and many other sources. A comparison of this work with the online *Oxford Dictionary of National Biography* for a random selection of Baptists or their associates who died between these dates revealed that while the majority of those entered in Boase' work are also entered, and much more fully, in the *ODNB*, there are yet some lesser known or even prominent Baptists who have entries in *Modern English biography* but not in the *ODNB*. These include Robert Hall Baynes (1831-1895), J.P. Chown (1821-1886), John Gadsby (1809-1893), Joseph Jackson Goadby (1828-1898), Thomas Goadby (1829-1889), Frederic William Gotch (1807-1890), James Hoby (1788-1871), William Landels (1823-1899), James Philippo Mursell (1799-1885), Samuel Rowles Pattison (1809-189?), Charles Stovel (1799-1883) and Frederick Trestrail, (1803-1890). It is therefore worth consulting this work if you know the subject of your research died in the latter part of the nineteenth century but does not have an entry in the *ODNB*, which should always be checked first.

For Wales, Scotland and Ireland in general there are the *Dictionary of Welsh biography*[277] and its supplementary volume[278], the *Dictionary of Scottish biography*[279] and *Chambers Scottish biographical dictionary*[280], and *A dictionary of Irish biography*[281], among others. The *Dictionary of Welsh biography* is of particular use for the many Welsh Baptist ministers whose influence extended across the border into England, but who are not included in standard general biographical dictionaries, such as the *ODNB*. A random check of a few Welsh Baptist names revealed that while the most illustrious of them, such as Caleb Evans (1737-1791), Christmas Evans (1766-1838), John Evans (1767-1827), Vavasor Powell (1617-1670), Joshua Thomas (1718/19-1797), Timothy Thomas (1753-1827), (only included within his father's entry), and Timothy Richard (1845-1919) are in the *ODNB*, many others are not, for example two Benjamin Evans (1816-1886) and (1844-1900), the two earlier Caleb Evans, (1676-1739) and (d.1790), two Hugh Evans (d.1656) and (1712-1781), Thomas Shankland (1858-1927), Benjamin Thomas (1836-1893), Morgan Edwards (1722-1795), Gethin Davies (1846-1896) and David Oliver (fl. 1785-1814). The Scottish and Irish biographical dictionaries mentioned do not have nearly such a wide coverage as the Welsh volume: they are much shorter and do not seem to include many Nonconformist ministers, or mention the denomination of biographees included for other reasons, although the *Chambers Scottish biographical dictionary* does have a subject index to the entries, including a heading "Religion".

With regard to more specifically Baptist biographical sources a useful general guide for family historians is Geoffrey Breed's *My ancestors were Baptists*[282], published by the Society of Genealogists. This helpfully gives the volume and page references for lists of Baptist ministers in Rippon's *Baptist Annual Register*, mentioned above, and the *Baptist Magazine*, as well as listing the local Baptist church records held in a number of repositories. The parallel publication *My ancestors were English Presbyterians or Unitarians: how can I find out more about them?*[283] contains some pointers towards sources for those General Baptists who moved towards Unitarianism, i.e. the General Baptist Assembly, as opposed to those who joined the New Connexion, as well as early General Baptists prior to their division.

As mentioned above, the obituaries of Baptist ministers published in the *Baptist Handbook* and, in years prior to its publication from 1861, in the *Baptist Magazine*, can now be located through the online index on the Baptist Historical Society's website, http://www.baptisthistory.org.uk. However, ministers who had gone abroad or left the denomination prior to their death did not receive a published obituary in the *Handbook*, although their career can often be traced until the time of their departure through its annual ministerial list. General Baptist ministers, and sometimes other members of their families or significant lay members of General Baptist churches, often received obituaries in the *General Baptist Magazine*, but there is unfortunately no overall index to these as yet, just as there is no composite index to the obituaries in the *Baptist magazine* after 1861, the *Baptist Messenger* or any of the other 19th century periodicals containing Baptist obituaries. The Strict Baptist Historical Society's Library maintains a list of Strict Baptist ministers, with references to published obituaries in the Strict Baptist periodicals (an early copy of which is kept in the Angus Library) and a selection of biographies (for details see the society's website at http://www.strictbaptisthistory.org.uk). It should also not be forgotten that prior to the publication of these specifically Baptist periodicals some obituary and biographical material relating to Baptist ministers can be found within such more general periodicals as the *Evangelical magazine*[284] and the *Gentleman's magazine*[285]. A useful guide to those in the latter has been produced by Alan Ruston[286].

The weekly newspapers *The Baptist Times*[287] and its predecessor *The Freeman*[288], have always published obituaries, both of ministers and missionaries and of significant lay Baptists. These can often be hard to locate, frequently being published some considerable time after the death of the person, there being no overall, and most of the time no

annual, index to these volumes, which stretch from 1855 to the
present day.

W.T. Whitley's manuscript card index of Baptist ministers in the
Angus Library can sometimes help to locate obituaries in periodicals,
but the cards can be both hard to read and frustratingly difficult for
identifying the sources used. They can nevertheless provide useful, if
not always entirely accurate, pointers towards relevant dates. The
same can be said for Whitley's *The Baptists of London*[289], which is an
otherwise useful source for identifying Baptist churches and their
ministers in the London area. Similarly, the Baptist histories
mentioned above can often provide useful biographical information
about ministers (an index to the personal and place names in Ivimey's
History of the English Baptists [58] was compiled by K.W.H. Howard in
1981 [59]). The name indices to the *Baptist Quarterly* and the
Transactions of the Baptist Historical Society can also be useful in
finding articles about individual Baptists: for details of how to obtain
copies of the cumulated indices as text files on CD-Rom see
http://www.baptisthistory.org.uk/basicpage.php?contents=publication
s&page_title=Publications#quarterly. They are also available for
reference viewing in the Angus Library.

The Dr Williams's Library in London holds the original lists of
dissenting congregations in England and Wales by counties, with
names of ministers, compiled by the Presbyterian, Dr John Evans, in
1715, as well as those by the Baptist Josiah Thompson, compiled in
1773. These are both of particular value in eighteenth century
research. An index to the Evans list has been published as Dr
Williams's Library Occasional Paper no. 11[290], and a transcript of the
Thompson list was published in the *Transactions of the
Congregational Historical Society*, vol. 5[291]. The Dr Williams's
Library also holds the C.E. Surman Card Index of biographical details
of dissenting ministers, which is in the process of being digitized and
made available online. Dr David Wykes, Director of the Dr
Williams's Trust and Library, states of it:

"it is an index of Congregational and English Presbyterian
ministers. It does contain many eighteenth and nineteenth-
century Unitarians because of the difficulties in identifying
doctrinal positions. There no doubt are some Baptists in the
index because of the movement of ministers between the
denominations, but it would be misleading to say it includes
Baptists. Surman's sources were almost entirely printed. It is
valuable because he searched so many of the denominational
periodicals (Evangelical Magazine, Christian Reformer) as well
as DNB, denominational historical journals, Yearbooks, etc,
but he did not include VCH or county sources. It does not
include the Evans List (except through citing James's very
inadequate transcription) and the information from the
Thompson List is from the transcript in the Transactions of the
Congregational Historical Society."[292]

Another useful eighteenth century list containing biographical
information about both Particular and General Baptist ministers, was
compiled by the Baptist minister John Collett Ryland in 1751, in the
Warwick Baptist Church Minute Book: a transcript of this was
published in the *Transactions of the Baptist Historical Society*, vol.
6[293]. The *Transactions of the Baptist Historical Society* also included
the useful 'An index to notable Baptists whose careers began within
the British Empire before 1850'.[294]

The reports and magazines of the Baptist colleges are another useful
source of biographical information. A minister's career can often be
traced through these, as most of the reports list the current
whereabouts of ministerial alumnae, and usually also note the year of
their death. The more renowned alumnae may even qualify for an
obituary in the college's report. The Angus Library contains a
selection of these reports, but the individual colleges probably hold
more complete sets of their own reports, as well as indexes to their
former students. When searching for college reports it is important to
remember the various amalgamations and changes of name. Details of

the Horton, Rawdon, Manchester and Midland predecessors of the present day Northern Baptist College can be found in Peter Shepherd's history of the college[295] and a brief earlier history of the Midland Baptist College[296], while the forerunner of Spurgeon's College at the Pastors' College at Metropolitan Tabernacle, and of Regent's Park College at Stepney Academy are described in published histories of these institutions[297] [298] [299] [300]. The Welsh colleges have particularly involved ancestries, the South Wales Baptist College at Cardiff stemming from the colleges at Abergavenny, Pontypool and Haverfordwest[301], and the North Wales Baptist College at Bangor originating at Llangollen[302]. Histories of Bristol Baptist College are also a rich source of information about ministers who had trained there[303] [304], as is Roger Hayden's published thesis *Continuity and change*[305]. Derek Murray has written a history of the Scottish Baptist College[306], while Joshua Thompson's works provide some information about Irish ministerial training [87] [88]. For details of the colleges' archival records and present day websites for contact details see section 5(d)(iv) below.

(The Bodleian Library, Oxford, Clarendon Building. RAM)

(vii) Theses and dissertations

It goes without saying that those beginning serious academic research
will wish to consult the results of the research of others into related
topics. Access to UK universities' dissertations and theses is being
revolutionised in 2009 as a result of the EThOS (Electronic Theses
Online System) project, which will allow individuals to find, access
and archive e-theses that are produced in UK Higher Education
institutions. For this purpose a UK database of theses is being
established at a 'Central Hub' at the British Library. Researchers will
be able to find theses via EThOS and download any of the 12,000 full
text theses that are already stored there. Any researcher who wishes to
read a thesis from another UK higher education institution may use

the system and download one of these 12,000 full text theses, or make a request for a thesis that is not yet digitised. EThOS was developed with generous funding from JISC [the Joint Information Systems Committee], CURL [Consortium of University and Research Libraries] (now RLUK [Research Libraries UK]) and the partners including The British Library and several UK Higher Education institutions led by Glasgow and Imperial: full details can be found at http://www.ethos.ac.uk/EThOS_The_Facts.html.

Until the creation of EThOS the chief online sources to locate theses and dissertations have been

Index to Theses (subscription required)
http://www.theses.com/

UMI Dissertation Services (institutional subscription required)
http://www.umi.com/products_umi/dissertations/

These are the online versions of the *Aslib Index to Theses*[307] and *Dissertation Abstracts International*[308]. It is always worth carefully assessing your search strategy when looking up relevant theses in these databases, by reading the Help pages and carefully formulating your search in advance, in order to achieve the maximum relevance. Theses on British history can also be found listed by the year completed, from 1995 to 2007, with theses in progress for 2008, on the Institute of Historical Research site at http://www.history.ac.uk/ihr/Resources/Theses/. The published version of *Historical Research for Higher Degrees in the UK* is issued each year in May[309]. Theses completed and theses in progress are prepared from information supplied by university registrars, secretaries of faculty boards and heads of departments, so the comprehensiveness or otherwise of the lists depends on the diligence of these authorities, in particular with regard to relevant theses completed in cognate non-History departments or in universities which have dispensed with departmental structures.

Some doctoral theses can also be found catalogued on their own
university's online catalogue, such as Oxford University's OLIS. The
copies of Oxford University D.Phil. theses which are kept in the
Angus Library as well as in the Bodleian Library are also catalogued
onto OLIS and can be consulted by appointment in the Angus Library.
They include a number of theses and dissertations on Baptist
historical and other theological subjects, compiled by students of
Regent's Park College and some others. A subject search of OLIS
should enable their retrieval. Some examples include those by
Land[310], McDonald[311], Robison[312], and Smith[313], while those of Horace
Russell[314] and Cawley Bolt[315] (the latter, like all theses at the Oxford
Centre for Mission Studies, which are validated by the University of
Wales, the Open University or the University of Leeds, is not a
University of Oxford D.Phil. thesis) are only available in the Bodleian
or the Oxford Centre of Mission Studies respectively. The University
of Wales also validates theses submitted from Spurgeon's College and
the International Baptist Theological Seminary. It is worth noting that
important research theses have been submitted for Master's degrees,
as well as for doctorates, such as that by Ruth Clifford[316], and these
can sometimes be even harder to identify and locate, unless they have
been sufficiently important to be published as monographs.

Edinburgh University describes how to search for one of its theses in
its library catalogue on
http://www.lib.ed.ac.uk/howto/findtheses.shtml. Other universities
may list recent theses and dissertations, and/or those in progress, on a
departmental website, such as the University of Keele, where history
theses of the last five years can be viewed at
http://www.keele.ac.uk/depts/hi/research/theses.htm, enabling one to
locate the theses of Anthony Cross[317], Kenneth Dix[318] and Michael
Nicholls[319], for example. Or Glasgow University, where Frank W.
Rinaldi's thesis on New Connexion General Baptists[320] can be found
by searching the theses section of its library catalogue at
http://eleanor.lib.gla.ac.uk/search~S7/, reachable from the
university's thesis service at http://theses.gla.ac.uk/.

Many doctoral theses have been published, often in a revised form and with the addition of an index. As noted in 4(b)(i) above many particularly useful publications for the student of Baptist history are those published by Paternoster in its series *Studies in Baptist history and thought, Studies in Evangelical history and thought, Studies in Christian history and thought* and *Paternoster Theological Monographs*, plus several published outside these series. Full details of current and forthcoming such titles can be found on the Paternoster website at http://www.authenticmedia.co.uk/AuthenticSite/Authentic/theology monographs studies%20in%20baptist%20history%20and%20thought /page/2, but most should also appear on such library catalogues as OLIS, COPAC and BL eventually.

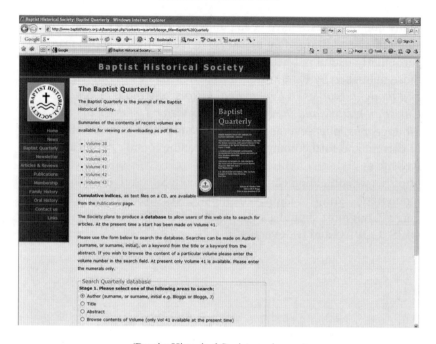

(Baptist Historical Society web page)

5. Primary sources

(a)   Digitized

Digital copies of primary sources can be found on the following
websites:

Digital Library of Classic Protestant Texts (institutional subscription
required)
http://solomon.tcpt.alexanderstreet.com/

Described as

"a uniquely exhaustive resource for historians, theologians, political scientists, and sociologists studying the religious and social upheavals of the 16th and 17th centuries, this comprehensive electronic collection gives researchers immediate, Web-based access to more than 1,200 works from the Reformation and post-Reformation eras. These works include the theological writings of more than 300 Protestant authors, as well as a wide range of confessional documents, biblical commentaries, polemical treatises, and Bible translations."[321]

It further describes its content thus:

"The Digital Library of Classic Protestant Texts debuted in the autumn of 2001. An ambitious undertaking, this robust electronic collection includes not only the principal works of the most eminent writers of the Reformation and post-Reformation eras, but also those of lesser-known authors of the period. Developed in consultation with an editorial board of the most eminent Reformation-period scholars in both North America and Europe, its comprehensive bibliography of sixteenth- and seventeenth-century Protestant writings has been revised and refined under expert guidance. Many of the books on it can only be found in the rare book rooms of the world's oldest libraries, such as the University of Oxford's Bodleian Library.

These invaluable biblical commentaries, catechisms, treatises, pastoral writings, sermons, church histories, disputations, and personal letters by Protestant writers, representing diverse theological perspectives, provide a sweeping view of the birth of early-modern Western Europe. ... The challenge levelled by Renaissance and Reformation scholars, "ad fontes," has been renewed and redefined to mean a return to the foundational sources of the Protestant Reformation."[322]

Its editorial selection criteria are given as follows.

"Works are generally published between 1500-1700.
Authors are all residents of Western Europe.
Documents are of a theological or religious nature.
Works display a broad representation of various theological
traditions.
Works include a wide array of document types.
Period editions are preferred.
First edition works have been selected unless scholars
determined that a later edition is more noteworthy."[323]

Early English Books Online (EEBO)
http://eebo.chadwyck.com/home

Many 17th century Baptist texts can be found, read and searched on
EEBO, but it is only available via an institutional subscription: owing
to its high cost smaller institutions are unlikely to have access to it.

It describes itself thus:

"From the first book published in English through the age of
Spenser and Shakespeare, this incomparable collection now
contains about 100,000 of over 125,000 titles listed in Pollard
& Redgrave's *Short-Title Catalogue (1475-1640)* and Wing's
Short-Title Catalogue (1641-1700) and their revised editions,
as well as the *Thomason Tracts (1640-1661)* collection and the
Early English Books Tract Supplement."[324]

Intute's description of it is:

"Early English Books Online (EEBO) is a digital collection of
over 125,000 books published between 1473 and 1700. Works
include: novels; prayer books; pamphlets and proclamations;
almanacs; calendars; and many other primary sources,

providing opportunities for research across: history; literature; religion; music; science; mathematics and the arts of Renaissance and seventeenth-century England. ... A powerful search engine enables the user to search fields including: author; title; printer; publication date; type of illustration; and Library of Congress subject heading. The results may then be viewed as scalable images, downloaded as PDF documents, or, in some cases, viewed as text files. Full bibliographic details are provided for each text. The resolution at which the books have been scanned is high, providing a good level of detail at some expense to download speed. Early English Books Online is a subscription service available to UK HE/FE institutions under a national license agreement negotiated by the Joint Information Systems Committee (JISC)."[325]

Eighteenth Century Collections Online *(ECCO)*
http://www.gale.cengage.com/DigitalCollections/products/ecco/index.htm
http://www.gale.cengage.com/pdf/facts/ECCO.pdf
Another source of digital text documents only accessible via institutional subscription is *ECCO*, which is now a part of Gale Digital Collections. Its public pages describe it as "the single most ambitious digitization project ever undertaken. It delivers every significant English-language and foreign-language title printed in Great Britain during the eighteenth century, along with thousands of important works from the Americas."[326] It allegedly makes use of "new technology that identifies subtle differences in the actual text as it appeared in eighteenth century literature", enabling researchers making use of the Advanced Search "by combining or excluding search terms, author, title, full text, front matter, main text, back-of-book indexes, publisher and place of publication," to

"pinpoint their searches and have more targeted results than a Keyword Search. A "fuzzy search" option expands the search to

include words similar to search terms entered, thereby
accommodating for spelling variations. ... All matching search
results are returned as citations. ... Researchers may click on
the citation title to access the work. Digital facsimiles, or
images of the book's pages are presented and may be viewed on
screen, saved (or marked) for later reference, printed and
InfoMarked for future use such as reading lists or directing
other researchers to this search."[327]

ECCO is divided into seven subject areas: History and Geography;
Social Science and Fine arts, Medicine; Science and Technology;
Literature and Language; Religion and Philosophy; Law; and
Reference, so, as with so many databases, items of relevance to
Baptist history may be included in either History or Religion, and
possibly also Social Science and Literature! The aim of the project
which created this database was to allow full-text searching of every
significant English-language and foreign-language title printed in the
United Kingdom between 1701 and 1800, along with thousands of
important works from the Americas and was based on *The English
Short Title Catalogue (ESTC)*.

Other e-books are being produced all the time, at a great rate, for
example in the Google Oxford project. These can usually be located
through the normal online library catalogues mentioned above. The e-
books themselves, however, will normally not be accessible outside
the universities holding subscriptions to the various providers.

Some more freely available, specifically Baptist, but largely American
sites with electronic versions of some key texts, or portions of them,
are noted below. It is worth being aware that some of these sites
collect and present their data to evidence a particular point of view.
Several of the websites mentioned above in sections 3 and 4(a)
provide links to original Baptist sources available online, in particular
The Baptist Observer's site at
http://www.yellowstone.net/baptist/history.htm.

Baptist Library Online
http://baptistlibraryonline.com

A specifically Baptist online source of digitized works, albeit from
only one Baptist tradition, **Baptist Library Online** is available without
a subscription. Intute describes it as follows:

> "The Baptist Library Online offers access to a range of
> important and hard-to-find texts by English and American
> authors in the Baptist tradition between the 17th and 19th
> centuries. The primary focus is on General Baptists and the
> Arminian (that is, free will) theology closely associated with
> them. Brief biographical information is included about key
> Baptist leaders whose work appears on the site, and a copy of
> the 1660 General Baptist Confession of Faith is available. Most
> texts are offered as PDF files – often facsimiles of printed
> editions – and HTML versions of many are also available. Also
> included is a short list of links to other related resources."[328]

The site's own welcome page describes its content thus:

> "You will find books here related to the General and Free Will
> Baptists. These writings date back to John Smyth and Thomas
> Helwys in 1611. They stem from the English General Baptist,
> American General Baptist and Free Will Baptist traditions."[329]

Center for Study of the Life and Work of William Carey, D.D. (1761-1834)
http://www.wmcarey.edu/carey/index2.html

This publicly available website includes an annotated bibliography of
works by and about William Carey, archival sources and web links, as
well as digitized copies of many works, both by Carey, including the
1792 text of the "Enquiry[330]" and by many of his associates, and of

periodical articles and notes relating to them and to the Baptist
Missionary Society: see
http://www.wmcarey.edu/carey/links/full_texts.htm. Also included
are many references taken from Cathcart's *Baptist Encyclopedia*[331]. It
also incorporates the extensive website on William Ward created by
Ronald Ellis: http://www.wmcarey.edu/carey/wmward/index.html and
provides links to many other websites with material on Carey.

Another huge list of websites, almost exclusively North American in
origin, comes from Phil Johnson, author of the 'Spurgeon Archive', at
http://www.spurgeon.org/~phil/bookmark.htm, with his own
assessment of them. The site's home page is at
http://www.spurgeon.org/ while the link to the Baptist page in "The
Hall of Church History" (which also incidentally includes an e-
version of *Foxe's book of martyrs*) is at
http://www.spurgeon.org/~phil/baptist.htm. This includes a large
number of links to Baptist sites, including quite a number of e-books.
One link is to "The Baptist Page" (last updated February 24, 2002!)
http://www.siteone.com/religion/baptist/baptistpage/main.html. The
site itself is not comprehensive, but his page of "Creeds, confessions
and catechisms" includes the texts of the London Baptist Confession
1644, Keach's Catechism 1677, the Baptist Confessions of 1689 (both
the original version, with links to the Scripture proofs, and
Spurgeon's edition), and the Philadelphia Confession of 1742, which
might be useful, although those with access to a library containing the
originals might wish to check their accuracy and completeness.

Yet another American site with transcripts of many Baptist documents
is the "Baptist History Homepage" at
http://www.geocities.com/baptist_documents/index.html with the
British documents listed separately at
http://www.geocities.com/baptist_documents/british.html. These
include a random collection of histories, biographies, Association
Circular letters, two of the famous composite portraits of Baptist
ministers and one of the BMS Jubilee (1842) medals. One link from

this leads to a partial transcription of the first volume of Ivimey's *History of the English Baptists* at http://www.vor.org/rbdisk/ivimey/html/index.htm#contents, with an index to the authors cited by Ivimey, compiled by M.T. Smith in 2004. For further transcripts of Baptist writings see http://www.baptisttheology.org/BaptistWritings.cfm, http://www.ageslibrary.com/ages_baptist_history_collection_1.html and other links from http://www.baptisttheology.org/ReadingsinBaptistHistory.cfm and http://www.baptisttheology.org/baptistresources.cfm.

Another American site which provides links to electronic copies of primary Puritan texts, is http://puritanism.online.fr/, which "contains resources on Puritanism in both Old and New England, and more particularly in early seventeenth-century Massachusetts"[332]. At http://puritanism.online.fr/primary_sources.html it provides a "Primary Sources Web Directory" on "English Puritanism and Puritan New England".

The Baptist Standard Bearer mentioned in 4(a) above also sells CD-Roms of important texts[333] and provides some primary texts by Gill and Brine as E-books[334].

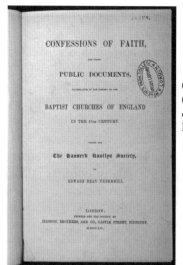

(Title page of Underhill, E.B. (ed.) *Confessions of faith and other public documents, 1854.* RPC)

(b) Facsimile or reprinted collections

Protestant nonconformist texts[335].

These 4 volumes, including the texts of original source documents from all the British nonconformist traditions, contain documents from the 17th, 18th 19th and 20th centuries respectively. The series note by the series editor Alan P.F. Sell states that "This series of four substantial volumes is designed to demonstrate the range of interests of the several Protestant Nonconformist traditions from the time of their Separatist harbingers in the sixteenth century to the end of the twentieth century. It represents a major project of the Association of Denominational Historical Societies and Cognate Libraries. Each volume comprises a General Introduction followed by texts illustrative of such topics as theology, philosophy, worship and socio-political concerns."[336] Each volume also contains a select bibliography of secondary sources and an index of personal names. What is noticeable, particularly in the early volumes, is that most of the documents are quoted from secondary sources or earlier reprints, such as those by Burrage[337] or Lumpkin[338], rather than from original source documents.

Baptist entries in volume one include John Smyth's "Short Confession of Faith in XX Articles", in the version printed in Lumpkin's *Baptist confessions of faith[339]*, Watts' *The Dissenters*[23] and Whitley's edition of John Smyth's works[340], excerpts from Thomas Helwys' *Mistery of iniquity[341]*, extracts from Bristol's Broadmead records (taken from Underhill's Hanserd Knollys edition[342]), from the Bedford Church Book, from John Bunyan and Samuel Fisher and a "theological miscellany" including extracts from the Baptist Confession of Faith of 1677, reaffirmed in 1688, and from the so-called "Gould" and "Kiffin" manuscripts taken from *Early English Dissenters* [but see notes below on these in Section 5(d)(vi)].

Volume two includes excerpts relating to Matthew Caffyn and the General Baptists, the Articles of Religion of the New Connexion General Baptists, an account of a Baptist ordination in 1794, excerpts from Caleb Evans, Christmas Evans, Benjamin Keach, John Gill, Andrew Fuller, William Carey (the "Great Commission" from the *Enquiry*[330]), the Bristol Education Society's "case for an educated ministry", plus various Association and church covenants.

Volume three includes many well-known nineteenth century Baptists, such as Robert Hall, William Gadsby, C.H. Spurgeon, Alexander Maclaren, Andrew Fuller, William Steadman, J.H. Hinton, Samuel Cox, John Clifford, John Rippon, Baptist Noel, J.C. Philpot, Frederick Trestrail, William Knibb, Dan Taylor. It also includes anonymous excerpts from every strand of Baptist life, such as the Baptist Union Declaratory Statement of 1888, the investigation into bankruptcy of Sir Morton Peto at Bloomsbury Baptist Church, 1868, "a Strict Baptist view of emigration, 1853", "a Baptist on Church Meetings, 1835", and "a Baptist view of the Baptism of the Holy

Ghost, 1810". By this century many of the excerpts are taken from the periodical literature.

The final volume includes from the Baptist constituency "The Baptist Doctrine of the Church, 1960", "The Baptist Understanding of Ordination, 1957", "Baptists and the Lord's Supper", John Clifford on the Boer War and on the End of the War, 1918, the "British Baptist message to American Baptists, 1917", "Shakespeare's vision of Free Church unity, 1918", "Baptists and the ten propositions, 1977" and a number of other extracts from Baptist documents.

These are all in general useful volumes for the juxtaposition of documents on related themes from the different nonconformist traditions, even if most of the extracts can easily be located elsewhere, but perhaps only if you know where to look.

Other British collections

Earlier collections of documents include the volumes *Victorian nonconformity*, edited by Briggs and Sellers[343], which contains excerpts from writings by Joseph Angus, John Clifford, Robert Hall, John Ryland, D.D. and C.H. Spurgeon among others, plus a section from the Minute Book of Pembroke Baptist Chapel, Liverpool, and *Nonconformity in the nineteenth century*, edited by David M. Thompson[344], while significant documents published by the Baptist Union of Great Britain and Ireland were reproduced and edited by Roger Hayden in 1980 as *Baptist Union documents, 1948-1977*[345]. Both the Hanserd Knollys Society in the nineteenth century and the Baptist Historical Society in the twentieth also published reprints of original documents[346] [347] [348] [349] [350] and [351] [340] [352] (the later *English Baptist Records* series is referenced under section 5(d)(ii) below). The *General Baptist Assembly Occasional papers*[353] include quite a number of transcripts from early General Baptist churches and private papers, mostly transcribed by the late Leonard Maguire: their contents

were listed in the *Baptist Quarterly* 40(3), July 2003. It should also
not be forgotten that both the *Baptist Quarterly* itself and its
predecessor the *Transactions of the Baptist Historical Society*, have
over the years contained transcriptions of many original manuscripts.
Additionally, quite a number of Baptist and related works have been
reprinted by the small Reformed publisher Tentmaker Publications
and local and family history societies often publish reprints of works
relevant to their interests.

American collections.

Earlier American published reprints of some significant Baptist
confessions of faith include Lumpkin's [338] and McGlothlin's[354]
volumes, while the number of reprinted collections of source
documents being published in the north American continent is rising
all the time. Useful examples include those by McBeth[355] and
Brackney[356], and Freeman, McClendon and da Silva's *Baptist roots[357]*.
Mercer University Press has also published reprints and transcripts of
Baptist writings in its Baptist Series, for example Thomas Helwys' *A
short declaration of the mystery of iniquity[358]* and Roger Williams'
The bloudy tenant of persecution for cause of conscience,[359] both
edited by Richard Groves, a series which includes the published and
unpublished writings of individuals, such as Anne Dutton[360] (see
http://www.mupress.org/webpages/books/baptistseries.html for other
titles) and in its Reprints of Scholarly Excellence (ROSE) series
(http://www.mupress.org/webpages/books/reprintsseries.html).

Another recent volume is *Readings in Baptist history*, by Joseph Early
Jr.[361]. a review of which can be found on the Baptist Theology
website[362]. In Canada Michael Haykin[363] and others[364] are publishing
edited reprints of Baptist works for the Particular Baptist Press[365] (see
http://www.pbpress.org/ for current publications and works in
progress).

(Title page of Underhill, E.B. (ed.) *Records of the churches of Christ, gathered at Fenstanton, Warboys, and Hexham, 1644-1720*. RPC)

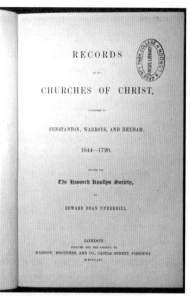

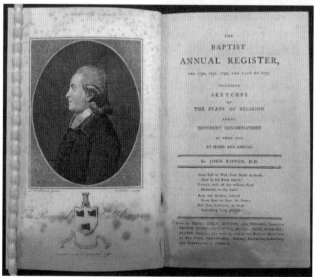

(Title page of John Rippon's *Baptist Annual Register of 1790*. RPC)

(c) Printed source documents

(i) Periodicals

For a general comment on my arbitrary division of Baptist periodicals into secondary and primary sources see the opening paragraph of section 4(b)(v) above.

The most useful survey and description of nineteenth-century Baptist periodicals is Rosemary Taylor's 1974 thesis, *English Baptist periodicals, 1790-1865*[366], the bibliography section of which, forming the first part of the thesis, was published in the *Baptist Quarterly* in 1977[367]. This is a very necessary source for those wishing to study any aspect of Baptist life and theology in the late eighteenth and early nineteenth century, because it lists in chronological order of the date of first issue all the periodicals known to have been produced between 1790 and 1865 by English Baptists, chiefly for members of their own denomination, and it also provides brief details of non-Baptist periodicals "which yet had strong Baptist connections". For each periodical the full title, subtitle and all variations of title are given, along with the numbering and dating, all the imprints and editors, size and price and an annotation which "sketches the character of each periodical with information of the following kinds: frequency of publication (when this is not mentioned in the title), type (e.g. miscellany, bulletin), ownership or official backing, sectarian grouping, readership, policy, contents, notable contributors, relations with other periodicals, and circulation."[368] Ken Manley's work on Rippon mentioned above, *'Redeeming love proclaim'*[245], also discusses religious periodicals contemporaneous with the *Baptist Annual Register*, many of which included some Baptists among their contributors[369].

The bibliography of Geoffrey R. Breed's *Particular Baptists in Victorian England*[370] also provides a useful list of periodicals. A list of the periodicals held in the Angus Library is available for

consultation within that library and may be available online in due
course or on request from the Librarian, while many of these
periodicals are in process of being catalogued onto OLIS. These
largely 19th century periodicals are of mixed value in providing
historically accurate accounts of events, originating as they do from
every possible sectarian group holding to Baptist principles. Indeed,
some groups were and even still are known by the name of the
periodical which they produce(d), such as the Gospel Standard
(Strict) Baptists. They are nonetheless useful source documents for
illustrating the outlook and opinions on many issues of the particular
group which published them.

The *Baptist Magazine*[247] (largely though not exclusively Particular
Baptist in its earlier years), the *General Baptist Repository* and
Magazine[371], the *Minutes of an Association of General Baptists [of
the New Connexion]* and its successor the *General Baptist Year Book*
[372], containing detailed reports from churches including membership
statistics right from its start in 1785, and Rippon's *Baptist Annual
Register*[244] are a mine of detail on Baptist churches, ministers, lay
people and the movements in general, as already described in section
4(b)(v) above, but also include original articles, letters and sermons,
often in their only published form. Rosemary Taylor's comment on
the *Baptist Magazine* describes it as a "monthly miscellany,
representing the main stream of Particular Baptists. Vols. 1-3 printed
at Tiverton; the management moved to London in 1812, and in the
same year the magazine gained the support of three influential
ministers in the provinces, Andrew Fuller, John Ryland and James
Hinton. Officially recommended in the constitution of the Baptist
Union 1813. Almost every notable Baptist Union minister of the
period contributed to it. In avoiding discord within the denomination,
it was often rather tame and dull, but it faithfully reflected the Baptist
consensus."[373] Later in the century in Scotland the *Scottish Baptist
Magazine*[374] and in Ireland the *Irish Baptist Magazine*[375] fulfilled a
similar function, with articles, reviews and news from the churches. It

is interesting to see that volume 14 for 1890 of the latter has an
engraved portrait of F.B. Meyer as its frontispiece.

The *Missionary Herald*[376], published both separately and as a
supplement to the *Baptist Magazine*, the *New Baptist Miscellany*, the
Primitive Church Magazine and the *Baptist Record,* and the *General
Baptist Missionary Observer*, published from 1822 only in the
General Baptist Repository and *Magazine,* provide full information
on the missionary work of the Baptist Missionary Society (then only
Particular Baptist) and the General Baptist Missionary Society
respectively until the Particular and General Baptists merged in 1891,
when the *Missionary Herald* took over all the missionary reporting.
The *Baptist Messenger*[377], subtitled *an evangelical treasury and
chronicle of the churches*, is another useful source, described by
Rosemary Taylor as a "monthly miscellany, containing short
devotional articles, sermons, historical sketches, serial stories,
denominational news, book reviews, poetry and, in the early volumes,
summaries of public events"[378].

There were many more periodicals, some only lasting for a few years
and often from one specific section of the Baptist community, which
contain a wealth of interesting information, as well as a commentary
on current affairs from their viewpoint. For example, Strict Baptist
periodicals containing details of churches, obituaries and similar
useful historical information, include the *Gospel Herald*[379] and *The
Earthen Vessel*[380], which later merged, and *The Gospel Standard*[381].
Some of the major theological controversies among Baptists of the
nineteenth century, such as the baptismal regeneration controversy,
the controversy about eternal life generated by Samuel Cox's *Salvator
mundi*[382] and the Downgrade controversy, were aired in the columns
of many of these periodicals. For periodicals as sources of church and
biographical information see sections 4(b)(v) and (vi) above.

The weekly newspaper *The Freeman*[288], later to become *The Baptist
Times*[287], mentioned above in the context of biographical sources

(section 4(b)(vi)), also contains fascinating details of Baptist life, although unfortunately there seem to have been only a few years when an index was produced, and it has not yet been digitized in searchable form, so considerable time needs to be set aside to search the bound volumes (or microfilms produced by the former Historical Commission of the Southern Baptist Convention[383]), if the information you require is the sort likely to be contained in it. Another periodical in newspaper format was *The Baptist*[384], which was only published over the course of a few years, before being amalgamated with *The Baptist Times and Freeman*.

While most of these periodicals are of use only for the nineteenth century, John Rippon's *Baptist Annual Register*, published from 1790 to 1802, reaches well back into the 18th century with some of the documents, minutes and proceedings which it published. As already mentioned, a thorough analysis of Rippon's *Register* has been compiled by Ken Manley in '*Redeeming love proclaim*'. His Table 5[385] shows, for example, that while in Volume 1 reports, letters and other material from the Associations took up 32.9% of the volume (186 pages) and American association material and correspondence 18.6% (106 pages), with obituaries, memorials 20.6% (116 pages) and material on missions 7.5% (42 pages), by volume 4 the proportions for these categories were 6.7% (40 pages), 8.6% (50 pages), 9.7% (57 pages) and 9.6% (56 pages) respectively. In their place miscellaneous anecdotes, sermons, extracts from rare books, devotional or theological articles in Volume 4 occupied 18.4% of the total (110 pages) as against 2.1% (11 pages) in the first volume, Intelligence (i.e. details of churches) now took up 8.4% (49 pages), compared with 1.2% (6 pages) in volume 1, and historical extracts, which had not been included at all in previous volumes, now took up 10.9% (65 pages).

(First page of *Northamptonshire Association Circular Letter* for 1768. RPC)

(ii) Association reports and circular letters

The whole body of reports and circular letters published by the area Baptist associations from the seventeenth century onwards is another valuable resource for Baptist historical research. In the seventeenth and eighteenth centuries these may have included a brief "state of the churches", but by the nineteenth century these had usually expanded to include detailed statistics of the churches in the Association, the names of ministers and messengers to the Association meetings, as well as news from the churches. These details can often be at least a year more up to date than those in the equivalent year of the *Baptist Handbook*. By means of these reports it may be possible to trace the history of a church, the career of a minister, or the course of denominational history in a region. The Circular letter (an annual letter from the Association to its churches, signed by the Moderator on behalf of the Association, but not usually written by him, the author's name often being noted in the Minutes or "Breviates" of the Association meetings, when the letter was read out) itself sometimes consisted of a history of the Association or of the churches in the Association. For example, in 1842 the Circular letter of the West-Riding of Yorkshire Association of Baptist Churches was "A brief historical account of the churches in the Association"[386]

What may be even more interesting for a study of the Association can be its credal statement at the start of each Circular letter, which may show significant changes over the years, which combined with changes in the list of churches represented in the Association can indicate theological rather than geographical reasons for a church leaving one Association to join another. For example, the 1768 Northamptonshire Association Circular letter begins:

> "The Circular letter from the ministers and messengers, assembled at Oulney in Bucks, June 15 and 16, 1768. Maintaining the important doctrines of three equal persons in the Godhead; eternal and personal election; the original guilt and depravity of mankind; particular redemption; free justification by the imputed righteousness of Christ; efficacious grace in regeneration; the perseverance of the saints in grace unto glory; and professing the primitive order and discipline of churches. To the several baptized churches of Christ whom they represent, meeting at Nottingham, Sheepshead, Arnsby, Foxton, Kettering, Walgrave, Northampton, Road, Oulney, Calton, and St. Albans."[387]

By 1800, the Northamptonshire Association's statement of faith had changed to:

> "... Maintaining the important doctrines of three equal persons in the Godhead; eternal and personal election; original sin; particular redemption; free justification by the imputed righteousness of Christ; efficacious grace in regeneration; the

final perseverance of real believers; the resurrection of the dead; the future judgment; the eternal happiness of the righteous; and everlasting misery of such as die impenitent; with the congregational order of the churches, inviolably;"[388]

By now there were twenty-two churches from nine counties in the Association, in contrast to the eleven from five counties in 1768 (with one, Calton, no longer listed), which demonstrates the increasing spread of the Northants Association far beyond the county boundaries of Northamptonshire. The subject and content of the actual circular letter can also often provide an indication of the theology of the Association.

With the changing structure of the Associations, and thus of their offices, it can be difficult to locate complete sets of these reports. There are quite a lot in the Angus Library, in the British Library and in other libraries in the British Isles and North America, but by no means complete sets, and while many published before 1800 have been catalogued on ESTC, and some are also now available electronically through *Eighteenth Century Collections Online (ECCO)* if your institution has a subscription to this, many have not yet been catalogued, let alone digitized, online. It is nevertheless worth checking COPAC for 18th and 19th century records, because the RSLP 19th Century Pamphlets project did succeed in prompting the cataloguing of quite a number of them both in the Angus Library and in various other CURL (now RLUK) libraries. Searching on the keywords "Baptist" and "Association" brings up quite a random selection of these reports from North America as well as the British Isles, but the search will need refining to limit it to those required, as 2896 records were retrieved using those keywords for publications between 1700 and 1899. OLIS alone retrieved 506 references, which were only reduced to 471 by limiting the search to publications between 1700 and 1900. The Appendix gives some examples of different methods of tracing Association reports and Circular letters.

(Tracts shelves in the Angus Library. RPC)

(iii) Tracts, sermons

Much the same can be said about locating the original works of many Baptist authors, when these were composed as tracts or independently published sermons. Thanks to the ESTC and the RSLP 19th Century Pamphlets project, many of those from the 17th to 19th centuries have now been catalogued by libraries contributing to COPAC and WorldCat, including many of the tracts published by the Baptist Tract Society (which have also been listed in their entirety in Appendix I of Geoffrey R. Breed's *Particular Baptists in Victorian England[389]*), but there are almost certainly many more in existence which have never yet been catalogued onto online databases.

Many libraries are no doubt in the same situation as the Angus Library, where there are still many volumes of tracts and sermons, often collected and bound by nineteenth century divines and relating to a topic dear to the collector's heart, which have not been individually catalogued in any form. Sometimes volumes directly relate to some particular topic or controversy, such as anti-slavery or the baptismal regeneration controversy, but many others, in the Angus Library at least, have very broad spine titles like "Tracts on baptism". A serendipitous search of the old Angus Library card catalogue under the word "Tracts" brings up the less than useful card "Tracts by

Baptist authors: several hundred, not individually catalogued, but bound alphabetically by authorship, the last three volumes being anonymous"[390]. Fortunately, most of the tracts in this particular set of volumes have now been catalogued onto OLIS. Another card with the heading "TRACTS" reads "A collection of fifteen in MS, undated and anonymous. Four of the Tracts are designed to show that no Baptism is valid but such as is received in Episcopalian churches"[391], a treasure trove which could perhaps not be located in any other way. Others have headings like "Five tracts for the thoughtful", "Six anonymous tracts" and "Ten Tracts on Christian baptism".

One volume located in the old card catalogue by the subject "Baptismal regeneration controversy"[392] has a typed note inside the front cover with the heading "Controversy on baptismal regeneration 1864-5" which reads "These documents were collected by a young deacon of Spurgeon's Tabernacle. He had them bound in about the year 1867. He presented them to Mr. Robert Stewart Thomson, who had done him a small service, prior to his death. Mr. Thomson was Financial Secretary of Dawes Road Baptist Church, Fulham. His son, Rev. Ronald W. Thomson, presented them to the Angus Library, 1980." This is typical of so many of these volumes, and I am sure the Angus Library is not unique in this. This volume contains tracts and sermons by a wide variety of authors, many of them in reply to C.H. Spurgeon, but there is no list of them inside the volume and none have as yet been catalogued individually online. Although some can be found via the secondary sources on such a topic as this, many may not yet have found the light of day and would repay serious study. Two other volumes located by the subject in the card catalogue have the spine titles "Spurgeon et al. Baptismal regeneration controversy"[393]. These have not been individually catalogued , but a helpful student/researcher on the subject has compiled a pencilled list of over sixty of the tracts in the volumes, the omissions presumably being those tracts unrelated to the topic.

Essays, tracts, sermons and discourses may have been collected for publication under the name of an author, such as those by Samuel Cox[394]: whilst many of these may not yet have found their way into online catalogues, the RSLP 19th Century Pamphlets and Revelation projects have enabled a large number to be located through COPAC. By contrast the prolific sermons of Charles Haddon Spurgeon, originally published in the *New Park Street*[395] then *Metropolitan Tabernacle Pulpit*[396] and innumerable collected volumes, have been repeatedly republished and reprinted, from Spurgeon's day to the present, as well as being copiously indexed and analysed.

Tracts from previous centuries are more likely to be accessible online in full text to those at an institution with a licence to EEBO and ECCO (see above). One such on ECCO is Samuel Hebden's *Baptismal regeneration disproved* of 1741[397]. Many seventeenth century tracts were published anonymously, but can often be traced online by title or subject keywords. In print form Whitley's *Baptist bibliography* contains a short index to anonymous works and in the Angus Library card catalogue many can be located via a significant word in the title, although most of these should by now be catalogued on ESTC and OLIS.

◢ The National Archives

(d) Manuscripts

(i) Guides

Clive Field's useful survey of nonconformist archives, *Preserving Zion,* [20] clearly sets Baptist archive records in the context of national collections of nonconformist archives in the UK as a whole, and his extensive bibliography provides details of such guides to these records as exist. Unfortunately, most of the general guides to nonconformist archives are either rather out of date, or seem strangely ignorant of Baptist records, largely because much of their research on Baptist records was conducted at Dr Williams's Library, if at all. This is the case with Mullett's *Sources for the history of English Nonconformity, 1660-1830* [21], which, while published in 1991, contains acknowledgements dated 1989, which explains the complete absence of any reference to the new Angus Library created in 1989 and the only reference to the Baptist Missionary Society Archives as being in London. It does not explain the absence of any mention of the church records from the Baptist Historical Society Library in the earlier Baptist Union Library, nor the use of excerpts from Baptist minute books largely held at Dr Williams's Library (by no means the largest repository of Baptist records) or from those published and in print. Even D.J. Steel's 1973 *Sources for nonconformist genealogy and family history* [398] mentions the old Angus Library and the Baptist Union Library and provides a useful, if by now outdated, general survey of nonconformist registers by Edwin Welch. Its bibliography too is useful for early works, including lists of congregations such as the Evans and Thompson lists noted in section 4(b)(vi) above, and some useful articles in archives and genealogy periodicals, even if its specific section on Baptists is limited.

The most useful relatively modern guide to nonconformist records is the Public Record Office readers' guide no. 13, by David Shorney: *Protestant nonconformity and Roman Catholicism: a guide to sources in the Public Record Office*[399], which describes the background to Old Dissent in the sixteenth and seventeenth centuries and explains civil registration in 1837, with reference to nonconformist baptismal, marriage and burial registers (even mentioning the discrepancy between births and baptisms in the case of Baptist baptisms), quoting from some Baptist registers and minute books. He also refers to the 1851 Religious Census and describes other nonconformist records, such as the registration of meeting houses, trust deeds, registers of nonconformist burial grounds and returns supplied by incumbents in 1831. Chapter 6 lists the various PRO classes relating to nonconformity and Roman Catholicism and a useful glossary is provided. The only errors with regard to Baptist collections are in the lists of "some other archive collections", which, while correctly placing the BMS Library at Didcot and its archives in the Angus Library, gives the Baptist Union Library as at Didcot and provides no reference to the main record collections of the Angus Library, even though the church records in the Strict Baptist Historical Society Library are listed correctly at Dunstable. The Baptist section of its bibliography is also limited and is unhelpfully given in paragraphs rather than as lists of titles.

Other pamphlets dealing with nonconformist records chiefly for family history purposes, such as those by Gandy[400] [401], McLaughlin[402], Palgrave-Moore[403] and Park[404], are extremely limited and often inaccurate in their treatment of Baptist records, for which by far the most detailed and useful guide is that by Geoffrey Breed already cited, *My ancestors were Baptists*[282]. Guides produced by individual Record Offices to the nonconformist records in their care can often be particularly useful, such as those from the Hertfordshire[405] [406],

Leicestershire[407], and Surrey[408] Record Offices, even though most can no doubt now be identifiable online, as can even those from some local family history societies, such as that from Northamptonshire[409].

Sources for Researching Nonconformists in Northamptonshire by Graham Ward

Available from the **Northamptonshire Family History Society** bookstall for £2.50 plus postage (UK 45p, airmail £1.40) ISBN 1904460275, Published November 2004.[410]

This new publication is a research guide to the complex area of nonconformist history with particular reference to Northamptonshire. By 1851, 28% of the county's population attended a nonconformist chapel, so it is likely that pan of your family will be involved with one of these groups. This booklet will help you to understand the different records that are available for research into nonconformity in the county. Topics include: background and historical context, sources for people and places, a brief overview of the different denominations, details of non-conformist libraries and societies plus a detailed bibliography and list of the non-conformist registers held at Northampton Record Office.

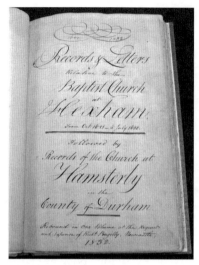

(Manuscript title page of Hexham and Hamsterley Church records rebound by Richard Pengilly 1832. RPC)

(ii) Local church records and how to find them

For Baptist churches of all persuasions the 'Church Book' is the primary source for historical research about an individual church or the people connected with it – minister, "messengers" in earlier years, elders, deacons (quite different from Anglican brethren with this title), and members. It usually contains the minutes of the Church Meetings (the general policy decision-making body in a Baptist church, consisting of all the baptised members of the church), including applications for baptism and membership, and frequently contains lists of members at certain dates and even records of births, marriages and deaths in some instances. This was sometimes the reason for the non-surrender of pre-1837 registers not found among the 'Non-Parochial Registers' in the Public Record Office: because such lists were embedded in the general church record the congregation was unwilling to surrender all the records of its history to a public body. Other useful church records can be the minutes of deacons' meetings, Sunday School minutes and the records of other associated youth organisations, church accounts and other aspects of the institutional church, although sadly all too often many of these have been lost.

The records which survive are kept in a wide variety of locations: many have been retained by the church itself, often under conditions which do not bode well for their chances of survival; some have been passed to the local Baptist Association for safe keeping (although with the recent changes in the Associations many of these have again been moved); some (more now, one hopes, than in 1991 when I first wrote this) have been deposited with the local County or City Record Office (or with a neighbouring County Record Office, if county boundary changes apply, as in the case of Berkshire and Oxfordshire, or if the records were with a trust handled by a solicitor working across county boundaries); some, deposited originally with the Baptist Historical Society or the Baptist Union, are now in the Angus Library and others have been deposited directly with Regent's Park College and the other Baptist theological college libraries. Many of those from the North-West of England deposited with the Northern Baptist College or its predecessors now form part of the Northern Baptist College Collection in the John Rylands University Library of Manchester.

The Baptist Union Corporation[411] holds the Deeds and Title of several thousand church properties and correspondence files concerning churches going back many years. A considerable amount of historical archive material in the form of related minute and account books was discovered in the Corporation's possession during the course of the Baptist Union move to Didcot in 1989 and afterwards and was forwarded to the Angus Library, apart from duplicate marriage registers received from the Registrar General for many years, which were distributed by the British Records Association to the appropriate County Record Office.

A number of early General Baptist church records are in Dr Williams's Library and there are collections of Strict Baptist

churches' records in the Strict Baptist Historical Society's library in
Dunstable (see http://www.strictbaptisthistory.org.uk/library.htm) and
the Gospel Standard Baptist Library at Hove. These last two
collections are listed in *My ancestors were Baptists*, mentioned above,
as are those in the Angus Library and Dr Williams's Library and in
the RG4 section of the Public Record Office. Edited transcripts of
some church records have been published, such as those published by
the Hanserd Knollys Society[342 412] in the nineteenth century, and the
Broadmead, Bristol records edited by Roger Hayden[413] and the first
two of the Baptist Historical Society's series of *English Baptist
Records*[414 415] in the twentieth.

Although the advent of the Internet and the online resources of the
National Archives[416] have made it much easier to locate local Baptist
church records, the autonomy of the local Baptist congregation and its
resistance to any form of central organization or authority have still
made for peculiarly Baptist problems in the storage, handling and
location of local records. Although advice can and has been given to
local churches by the Baptist Historical Society, the Baptist Union
and the Associations as to what to do with their records, there is no
authority, as in some other denominations, to require the deposit of
certain types of records, with, for example, a local County Record
Office or a Baptist College library. Tracing these records, if they have
not found their way into a public repository or responsible library, is
therefore not easy, in particular in the case of extinct churches. The
Angus Library holds the responses to the Baptist Union's 1961 and
1984 surveys of the whereabouts of churches' records, at which time
many were still in the hands of the local Church Secretary, but far
more churches did not respond than did. Similarly, arrangements have
been made between the Angus Library and a number of record
repositories to exchange lists of Baptist/local records which each
holds, although the need for this will lessen as the catalogues of the
National Archives become more complete. If local churches can
always inform the Angus Library when they have deposited their

records somewhere it will help to bring these sources of information up to date.

Access to Archives (known as A2A) "allows you to search and browse for information about collections of records (archives) in England and Wales, dating from the eighth century to the present day. The archives described on A2A are cared for in local record offices and libraries, universities, museums and national and specialist institutions across England and Wales, where they are made available to the public. To find out whether archives are of interest to you, it is necessary to consult a catalogue or other finding aid. A2A allows you to search across detailed catalogues from around 400 record repositories in England and Wales beyond The National Archives at Kew, so you may arrange to see or to obtain copies of genuine historical documents with just a few clicks of your mouse".[417] You can search by keyword (beware the word 'Baptist' will retrieve a lot of Anglican churches dedicated to St. John the Baptist), by reference, by repository (which you can identify through the ARCHON directory) and by date.

The National Register of Archives, on the other hand, which is maintained by The National Archives: Historical Manuscripts Commission, "provides information on the nature and location of manuscripts and historical records relating to British history". Its indexes offer a means of searching the catalogues and lists held within the NRA, which can be consulted in The National Archives' Reader Enquiries Room.

("The NRA, as a collection of catalogues and lists, was established in 1945. It developed out of the Reports and Calendars, which the Royal Commission on Historical Manuscripts had been producing since its formation in 1869. The Reports and Calendars were originally produced to provide a survey of the nature and location of records relating to British history held in private hands throughout Britain. It was, in part,

because of the extent of the material collected that the
Historical Manuscripts Commission formed the NRA as a
source for maintaining catalogues and lists. In 1995 the indexes
of the NRA were made available online. Since then as more and
more catalogues and lists have been made available
electronically the indexes have provided links to electronic
catalogues. The material in the NRA is collected in a number of
ways: lists of records produced by institutions and
organizations are sent to The National Archives: Historical
Manuscripts Commission, staff researching in their fields
uncover material previously unknown and accession reports,
which are collected annually, all provide sources of information
that is entered into the indexes of the NRA. The National
Archives continues to map the location of manuscripts and
records today as a result of the movement of records and, more
importantly, because material is continually being produced
and discovered. Records relating to British history are also
regularly found in repositories throughout the world and are
noted in the indexes of the NRA.")[418]

"The National Archives has developed a new Global Search
which allows you to search the Catalogue at the same time as
the Access to Archives (A2A) database, DocumentsOnline and
other online resources. Global Search is a one-stop search
across the holdings of The National Archives of the United
Kingdom and of local and private archives (mostly in England)
delivering fast results sorted by subject. Your results list will
tell you which database each hit came from. There will also be
a link to the catalogue entry, so you can follow up on your
findings. You can use the Advanced Search to select specific
databases."[419]

This will clearly be your first port of call when trying to locate the
records of an individual Baptist church. If the church is not listed in
these indexes the next step is to check in the current *Baptist Union*

Directory, often held in local public libraries, but otherwise available for consultation by appointment in the Angus Library, to see if the church is still in existence, and if so, to find the name and address of the Church Secretary, who may be able to tell you where the older records of the church are kept (or, unfortunately, may well not). This Directory will also give details of the regional Association to which the church belongs, which again may or may not have information relating to the whereabouts of the church's records. If the church has closed and there is no reference to it in the above National Archives catalogues it is worth checking the local Record Office anyway, as it may not yet have contributed all its indexes to the national online catalogues. You can then consult the Angus Library at angus.library@regents.ox.ac.uk which may have a note relating to the church's closure, or some other hint which could help to locate the records. None of these sources are foolproof, however, and many older Baptist records have simply been lost or destroyed. Some early General Baptist records can also be located on the Unitarian Historical society's "Location list of records" of English Presbyterian/General Baptist/ Unitarian congregations in Great Britain at

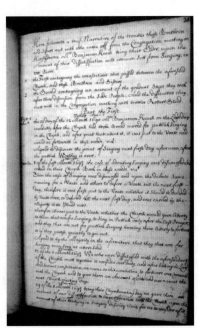

(Maze Pond Church Book, 1691-1708. RPC)

http://www.unitariansocieties.org.uk/historical/hsrecords.html, although this does not seem to include the General Baptist records from London and Kent in the Angus Library, which complement and in some cases complete those in Dr Williams's Library and the Guildhall Library.

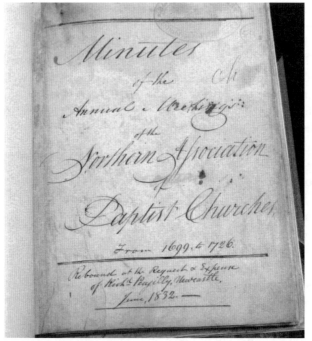

(Title page of *Northern Association minutes, 1699-1726*,
rebound Pengilly 1832. RPC)

(iii) Association and other organization records

After the records of local Baptist churches those of the regional
Associations may be of interest for historical purposes. The printed
reports and circular letters have been mentioned above, but there are
also various manuscript records originating from the Associations.
From an early stage in Baptist church history, at least the 1650s,
individual Baptist churches made contact with others of a similar
persuasion in their vicinity and these informal contacts were soon
formalised into regular Associations, or, as John Briggs has put it,
"Very early in Baptist life the need to complement the congregational
principle by a pattern of association had been readily perceived"[420].

The earliest records of the meetings between the 'messengers' were often kept in one or more of the individual Church Books: an edited transcript of some of these by B.R. White was published by the Baptist Historical Society as *Association records of the Particular Baptists of England, Wales and Ireland to 1660*[421]. Similarly, Stephen Copson's aforementioned work on the Northern Association[180] includes a transcript of that association's early records. By the eighteenth century letters between the churches, accounts of the Association meetings and details and statistics of the churches in an Association in the form of an annual report were being kept for most Associations and many survive in manuscript form. (For a description of the distinction between the Associations founded in the seventeenth century and those which came to life after the Evangelical Revival in the eighteenth century see Geoffrey Nuttall's chapter 'Assembly and Association in Dissent, 1689-1831'[422] in *Studies in Church history*, vol. 7. The nineteenth century pattern is described in much greater detail by John Briggs, in the work cited above, chapter 7, 'Associations, alliances and the wider church'.[423])

A few of these early Circular Letters are in the Angus Library, such as those of the Midland Association addressed to Bewdley Baptist Church[424] and a number of other Association records - minutes, correspondence, details of churches, etc. - have also been deposited in the Angus Library, more since the recent changes in Association names and jurisdictions, but there is no central file showing the whereabouts of early Association records. As with church records, those deposited with local repositories should have found their way onto A2A (a search of which produced 144 results for the phrase "Baptist Association", which include collections deposited by a local Baptist Association and references in a church's records to attendance at Association meetings as well as the actual records of a regional Baptist Association), but many others will not yet have been listed. It is worth checking directly first with the present day successor Association(s), then with the relevant County Record Offices, of which there may be several which could have been in the area represented by the Association concerned, with any local studies library, with the Angus Library and any other possibly relevant Baptist college library and finally with Dr Williams's Library, particularly if it is an old General Baptist Association's records which are required, although these should now be recorded on the NRA.

Alongside the local Associations other assemblies, societies, boards and organizations soon grew up, whether from a group of like-minded ministers meeting in an eighteenth-century London coffee house or from a felt need for wider cooperation and discussion of issues of mutual concern. All these organizations produced records and correspondence, some of which have survived and some of which in turn have been catalogued. Of singular importance in the study of Baptist history are the minute books of the Particular Baptist Fund, now on deposit in the Angus Library[425]. This Fund was established in 1717 as a result of the response to a 'Proposal for raising a Fund' contained in a letter sent out to Particular Baptist churches in and about London proposing:

> "that a Public Fund, or Stock, be raised … for the support and maintenance of honourable Ministers, and providing for a succession of such. That this Fund shall be for the use and advantage of those Churches only that go under the denomination of Particular Baptists. That it be begun by taking subscriptions and making a public collection for it in the several congregations of that persuasion in London and the parts adjacent, and by the free gift of any particular persons whom God hath blest with an ability and disposition for such an extensive and pious charity … "[426]

The Particular Baptist Fund is still in existence and a brief history of it can be found on its website http://www.pbfund.org.uk/history.html. A new history of the Fund is being compiled by Allan Tribe, to be published for the Tercentenary in 2017. The lists of ministers, churches and colleges helped by the Fund from its foundation until

1975, as well as the discussions of the principles involved in making allocations, all contained in the Minutes, are a rich source of denominational history. A similar Fund, the Bristol Baptist Fund, of smaller financial resources, was formed in Bristol in the same year as the Particular Baptist Fund was founded, 1717: an account of it is given in a pamphlet published in 1958[427].

There is also an agreement between Regent's Park College and the Baptist Union of Great Britain that its Council and main committee minutes up to thirty years past should be deposited in the Angus Library, with the result that there is now a complete set of BUGB(I) minute books there from 1812 to 1975[428].

Other Baptist organizations whose occasional minute books are in the Angus Library include the Society of Baptist Ministers in London (General Baptist)[429], the General Baptist Building Fund[430], the Conferences of New Connexion General Baptists[431], the Baptist Board[432], the Baptist Monthly Meeting[433], the London Baptist Property Board[434], the London Association of Strict Baptist Ministers and Churches[435], the London Baptist Preachers' Association[436] and the Baptist Irish Society[437]. The single extant volume of minutes of the Baptist Itinerant Society for 1797-1812[438] is contained within the BMS Archive on deposit in the Angus Library (see below).

Outside the UK significant international Baptist institutional archives, in addition to individual countries' own institutional records, are those of the Baptist World Alliance and the European Baptist Federation. The former are mostly now in the USA in the recently moved American Baptist Archive Center in Atlanta, Ga., see http://abhsarchives.org/about.shtml, (apart from some early records in the Angus Library) and the latter now housed in the library of the International Baptist Theological Seminary in Prague. Details of the BWA archive collections can be found in its published history mentioned in section 4(b)(ii) above[439], while the list of the EBF archives now in Prague prepared by Alec Gilmore, an old typed version of which is in the Angus Library, has not yet been published, although the new history of European Baptist beginnings by Ian Randall to be published in 2009 [152] will refer to the EBF Archives.

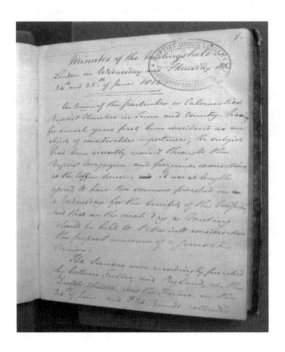

(First page of first *Baptist Union minute book*, 1812. RPC)

(Engraving "Baptist College, Stepney". RPC)

(iv) Baptist colleges' records

The archives of the Baptist colleges, the printed reports and histories of which have been mentioned briefly in 4(b)(vi) above, will also repay study, initially in consultation with the college's Librarian and/or Archivist. Bristol Baptist College has an Access database as well as a card index for its alumni, but this is not publicly available so enquirers should contact the Librarian in the first instance. It also has photographs of students from the late 19th century to the present day, which are in albums and can be searched by year of graduation and then alphabetically by student name. If a student did not graduate he could probably be traced on the group photographs. Those from recent years are also in a digital format, but there are no plans to digitize the older ones at the moment. Contact details for the college are on its website at http://www.bristol-baptist.ac.uk/.

The minute books of the former Midland Baptist College (General Baptist), later incorporated into what became the Northern Baptist College, are in the Angus Library at Regent's Park College, the first volume as the minutes of the General Baptist Education Society, 1825-1861[440] and then as the minutes of the Nottingham Baptist College[441]. The later minutes of the constituent colleges of the Northern Baptist College are listed in Peter Shepherd's history of the college cited in section 4(b)(vi) above, which shows that those of Manchester Baptist College for 1874-1965 and of Rawdon College, as well as those of the latter day Northern College are kept in the Northern Baptist College Record Room[442]. Contact details for the College are on its website at http://northernbc.wordpress.com/.

Regent's Park College archives retained in the Angus Library contain committee and Council minute books from the mid-nineteenth century, from Joseph Angus' presidency, although not from the earliest Stepney College days (apart from the diaries of the first President of the college, William Newman[443]), along with considerable correspondence with Joseph Angus relating to students during the 1840s and 1850s. There is no composite index to all alumni of the last two hundred years, although annual reports did contain cumulative lists of all ministers trained at the college, with separate lists of lay students, unfortunately with no alphabetical index before the report for 1938-9. From then until the report for 1971-2 the reports list deceased Baptist ministers trained at the college chronologically by year of leaving college, while those still alive are listed alphabetically. The reports for 1972-3 and 1973-4 no longer include deceased alumni, only the alphabetical list of living alumni, with lay members included since the college became a Permanent Private Hall of the University of Oxford in 1956. From 1975 the annual report was no longer published in that format, the publication *Regent's Now,* which only lists the incoming and outgoing students of the current year, replacing it. Student records have been kept by the college administration since the mid twentieth century, first on manual index cards then later on electronic databases. Enquiries relating to former students from the nineteenth and early twentieth centuries should be addressed to the Librarian in the first instance, but for more recent students to the Principal's Executive Assistant (contact details on the college website at http://www.rpc.ox.ac.uk). The College Archives also contain a number of photographs and photo albums, but these have not yet been indexed in any detail.

Spurgeon's College has transferred the basic details of former students originally kept on index cards and a manual register onto a database, so that it is possible to search it by surname, name of church, country, etc., but it has not yet been edited for consistency or added to in recent years, since the data was simply copy-input from the register by a volunteer. This is in the process of being rectified, but it will not be accessible online to outside enquirers, who should contact the Librarian for information (details on the college website at http://www.spurgeons.ac.uk/). It also holds a collection of photograph albums containing photographs of the majority of 19th century students and many of the early 20th century students, which have been re-numbered and indexed onto an Excel spreadsheet. In addition, there is a series of group photographs of students from the late nineteenth century onwards, which have also been identified and indexed, so that it is possible to ascertain fairly easily if there is a photograph of an individual student. Many of these have been scanned so that an electronic copy can be sent to enquirers who contact the Librarian. Spurgeon's College also houses an extensive C.H. Spurgeon archive in a Heritage Room, with artefacts and correspondence. The former have been inventoried and indexed, but the many hundred manuscript letters both to and from C.H. Spurgeon have yet to be fully catalogued and indexed in detail.

The Welsh, Scottish and Irish Baptist Colleges should be contacted directly for details of their records (http://www.swbc.org.uk/ , http://www.northwalesbaptistcollege.org.uk/welcome.htm ,

http://www.scottishbaptistcollege.org/ , and
http://www.irishbaptistcollege.co.uk/ .

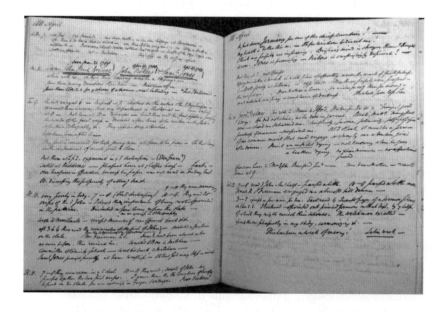

(William Newman's diary, volume for 1808-1814, Angus Library Z.k.1. RPC)

(The Mission House,
Kettering: engraved picture.
BMS)

(v) Baptist Missionary Society (BMS World Mission)

The main archives of the Baptist Missionary Society (now BMS
World Mission) dating up to thirty years previously were deposited
with the Angus Library in August 1989, at the time of the move from
London of both the BMS and the Baptist Union of Great Britain to
new joint premises, named Baptist House, in Didcot, Oxfordshire.
The organization's website is at http://www.bmsworldmission.org/
but details of the archive collection can be found on the Mundus
website, at http://www.mundus.ac.uk/ , by searching under the
organization name (as 'Baptist Missionary Society' or 'BMS'), where
access details for the Angus Library can also be found, as well as
other repositories holding some related papers (such as Stanley
Browne's papers in the Wellcome Library). The main BMS Archives
consist of both the committee minutes of the Society from its
foundation in 1792 and the correspondence, diaries and reports from
the missionaries overseas and the officers of the Society at home.
Brian Stanley's Bi-centenary history of the Society[444] provides full
background to the creation of these archives and its footnotes can act
as a useful index tool to the files, while its bibliography points to

relevant archive collections elsewhere and much useful background printed material.

Many of the papers are of wider interest than for the study of Baptist missions, such as George Grenfell's original survey books and maps of the Congo River[445], Roxburgh's Indian botanical work first printed and annotated by William Carey in Serampore[446], first-hand accounts of the Boxer Rebellion and later martyrdoms in China[447], the slave trade in the West Indies[448], and references in the correspondence of W.H. Bentley in the 1880s to Roger Casement[449], who was briefly employed by the BMS in his early days in Africa, and later correspondence between Casement as British Consul to the Congo with George Grenfell[450]. Extensive use of the BMS Archive has been made during the research for a number of significant publications, which include Catherine Hall's work on the Jamaica Baptist Mission, *Civilising subjects: metropole and colony in the English imagination, 1830-1867*[6], referred to by John Briggs in his editorial review in the *Baptist Quarterly* as "a large book of major significance to readers of this journal"[451] or Geoffrey Oddie's *Imagined Hinduism: British Protestant missionary constructions of Hinduism, 1793-1900*[7], with its chapter relating to William Carey and William Ward. (Details of reviews of these works and the search techniques required to find them can be found in Section 2(a) above.) The many other relatively recent works relating to William Carey whose authors have made considerable use of the BMS Archive include the Australian Keith Farrer's work *William Carey: missionary and botanist*[452], as well as Terry Carter's transcripts of Carey's journal and a selection of his letters[453].

Much of the pre-1914 material was microfilmed by the then Historical Commission of the Southern Baptist Convention, of which there is a summary catalogue[454], now accessible on the Southern Baptist Historical Library and Archives website at http://www.sbhla.org/downloads/mf_5350.pdf . Within the Angus Library there are detailed typed catalogues by country of the correspondence of missionaries whose association with the Society ceased before 1914. Many of these were recorded on the National Register of Archives and are available for consultation in the National Archives at Kew. The Regent's Park College Archivist is in the process of correcting and updating these. The Angus Library also holds a database of missionaries employed by the Society, which can be searched by name, date and range of dates, area mission field and mission station, home church, and college. This enables a search of, for example, the missionaries active in a particular country or mission station, or coming from a particular local church, during a specific range of dates, to be conducted and provides details of birth and death dates, links to spouses and other known relatives and references to published obituaries and other related library material. This too is being modernised. While post 1914 correspondence has not yet been fully catalogued, volunteers, under the direction of the Archivist, have been working for some years on detailed listing and piece-numbering of these letters, with the ultimate aim of providing a complete index to the Archive.

In addition to the Society's own Archive, there are within the collection some other useful historical documents collected by or given to the Society, such as the single minute book of the Baptist Itinerant Society for 1797 to 1812 mentioned above [438] or that of the General Baptist Missionary Society for 1816 to 1861 [455] (the Societies did not merge until the General and Particular Baptists united in 1891), a bound volume of letters to John Sutcliffe dated 1736-1779 [456], and the scrap book volume of contemporary manuscript and printed documents relating to the Down Grade controversy [457]. The BMS Archive also contains a large collection of photographic material, which has been sorted, boxed and indexed on an Access database, some old 35mm films and some filmstrips, coins, medals and other artefacts (including Robert Arthington's christening robe!), and an extensive collection of printed vernacular materials in a variety of oriental and African languages, including many biblical translations published by the Serampore Press, all of which have now been catalogued onto OLIS (http://library.ox.ac.uk/).

A number of other repositories hold significant archives relating to Baptist Missionary Society missionaries, most notably the School of Oriental and African Studies and the Wellcome Library in London, the John Rylands University Library of Manchester (see Timothy Whelan's calendar and notes on this collection in *Baptist Quarterly* 42(8))[458 463], Birmingham University's Special Collections Department http://www.special-coll.bham.ac.uk/ , the University of Edinburgh and the Henry Martyn Centre at Westminster College Cambridge, some of which can be identified and located through the Mundus gateway http://www.mundus.ac.uk/ . In addition, the North Yorkshire Archives Service at Northallerton holds a collection of Marshman papers in the Havelock Archive, not listed on the Mundus gateway but identifiable via the National Archives at http://www.nationalarchives.gov.uk/ (General Sir Henry Havelock married the daughter of Joshua and Hannah Marshman, BMS Serampore missionaries)[459] and the British Library holds letters of William Carey and other Serampore missionaries[460]. There are probably many more missionaries' papers in local repositories, which may also be identified via the National Archives website.

(BMS Centenary medal. BMS)

(First page of first BMS minute book.BMS)

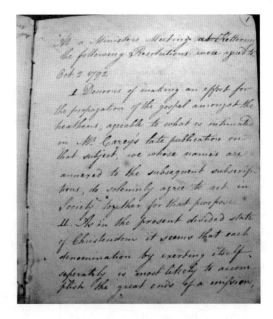

(vi) Miscellaneous manuscript archives

The correspondence and personal papers of many prominent Baptists have found their way into a wide variety of libraries and record repositories in the UK and overseas, as well as the national Baptist collection in the Angus Library at Regent's Park College, Oxford. Some of these have been calendared in the *Baptist Quarterly*, such as the 201 letters collected by Isaac Mann[461], now in the National Library of Wales at Aberystwyth, with a subsidiary collection of eighty-six more letters in the Osborn Collection in Yale University Library[462], or the Baptist autographs collected by Thomas Raffles and his son in the John Rylands University Library of Manchester, as noted above calendared (and in many cases also to be transcribed) by Tim Whelan [458 463]. Many other collections can be located through the catalogues of the National Archives, such as the Pashkov Papers in Birmingham University Library[464], the correspondence of M.E.

Aubrey with William Temple,
George Bell and others in the
Lambeth Palace Library[465], the
collected letters written to John
Rippon in the British Library[466],
those of John Ryland in the
Northamptonshire Record
Office[467], or the notes and papers
of C.B. Jewson and others in the
Norfolk Record Office[468], to
name but a random selection. It
is worth emphasizing the
importance of looking at the
search tips and other guidance
on websites such as those of the
National Archives, the British
Library or individual record
repositories, because they all
tend to be organized differently:
for example, how you search for

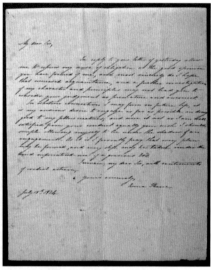

(Letter from Anna Pearce (to Jonathan
Carey) dated July 15th 1824. RPC)

personal or corporate names. It is very easy to miss relevant
documents merely by entering a name in the wrong field or in an
incorrect format.

The manuscript collections in the Angus Library include those of the
family of the hymn writer Anne Steele[469] (which, in addition to many
unpublished poems of Anne Steele, also contains poems of Mary
Steele of Dunscombe, including a manuscript of *Danebury Hill*
1768[470]); much of William Carey's personal and family
correspondence outside the BMS Archive[471]; the Angus family
archive[472]; the papers of Joseph Kinghorn[473]; those of J.H.
Rushbrooke[474]; and the letters collected by Dr Marjorie Reeves[475],
which are chiefly addressed to John Saffery from various individuals
at home and abroad, many of which relate to the Baptist Missionary
Society. Most of these have typed catalogues available for

consultation within the Angus Library, and most of them were also submitted to the National Register of Archives, and some are likely to be mounted in due course onto the Regent's Park College website at http://www.rpc.ox.ac.uk . From earlier centuries there are those manuscripts formerly referred to as the "Gould manuscript"[476], the "Stinton manuscript"[477], and the "Abingdon manuscript"[478]: for further references relating to these three see Larry Kreitzer's note in *Recycling the past or researching history[479]*. This is but a small sample of the manuscript archives contained within the Angus Library at Regent's Park College, collected during the college's 200 year history.

The other Baptist colleges also contain some significant archives, most noteworthy the papers of Charles Haddon Spurgeon at Spurgeon's College mentioned in section 5(d)(iv) above and of Dr John Ryland and others in Bristol Baptist College.

(First page of letter from
Joseph Angus to Thomas Raffles
dated 7th June 1844. BMS)

6. Conclusion

In conclusion, I would reiterate the importance of using all kinds of information resources when beginning your research, checking and rechecking all your search techniques, thinking outside the box when considering the interdisciplinary nature of Baptist history and remembering that there is still a lot of material out there, both printed and in manuscript, which has never even been catalogued or indexed electronically, let alone digitized and made available online. The Internet does nevertheless make your initial research much easier than in times past, as long as you remember that it is only a start and that the use of lateral thinking to identify other possible sources of information of relevance to you is always necessary.

(Engraving of Holford House, "The College, Regent's Park". RPC)

(Portrait of Dr John Ryland
(Regent's Park College. RPC)

APPENDIX

SAMPLE RESEARCH STRATEGY ON THE HISTORY AND THEOLOGY OF THE ENGLISH BAPTIST ASSOCIATIONS

1. First use the sources in section 4 above for the general **background to English Baptist history** in order to place Association history in context. Note the distinctions between the national General Baptist Association and Particular Baptist county or regional groups and also between the early Associations and those resulting from the influence of the Evangelical Revival (Nuttall[480] and Briggs[481]). Bear in mind too the fluid Strict Baptist scene, both in the nineteenth and twentieth centuries, with the emergence of Grace Baptists and churches which moved between Gospel Standard and Grace Baptists. In the nineteenth century churches practising strict communion were not always Strict Baptist.

2. Check **published work** in books and periodicals, completed **theses** and **research in progress** for any work already completed on the history of Baptist Associations as a whole, using online catalogues and databases.

3. Identify **current and past Association names**, using the links from the BUGB website for current associations: http://www.baptist.org.uk/baptist_life/baptist_family/regional/associat ions.html and following up historical notes on the individual Associations' websites where available. Find former Association names from the printed *Baptist Handbook* and *Baptist Union Directory*. Earlier *Handbooks* list Strict Baptist, General Baptist and unassociated churches as well as those in membership with the Baptist Union of Great Britain and Ireland. Some Associations included Baptist and Congregational churches, like the Bedfordshire Union of Christians. Modern non-geographical associations include the Old Baptist Union and Progressive Baptists, as well as those in partnership with Independent Methodists.

4. Use these names to search Google, other search engines, bibliographical websites and library catalogues; e.g. British Humanities Index and the RHS Bibliography, and indexes to periodicals, in particular *Baptist Quarterly* for reviews as well as articles, for any **published histories of or research on specific associations** and regions, searching under all variations of the Association name as a phrase. Locate copies of significant such histories from COPAC, WorldCat, library catalogues, Starr and Whitley's Baptist bibliographies and follow up references. There are unlikely to be many available in full text online, but it is worth checking library catalogues which show this.

5. Locate **primary sources** for the individual Associations, e.g. Association **Circular letters** and reports

a) Identify any digitized and available online using the names identified in 3 above;

b) Locate others from catalogues, e.g. ESTC, WorldCat, COPAC, but N.B. many are not yet catalogued online;

c) Search the Angus Library, other Baptist college libraries and Dr Williams's Library card catalogues;

d) Check Starr and Whitley's *Baptist Bibliographies* – slow but necessary;

e) Check *Baptist Annual Register* and 19th century periodicals for Association reports, using Rosemary Taylor's thesis to identify useful pre 1865 periodicals and working systematically through the main series, e.g. *Baptist Magazine, General Baptist Magazine, Earthen Vessel*, etc.

f) Locate **manuscript Association records** in County Record
Offices and other repositories, searching A2A and the NRA
through the National Archives website;

g) Locate early Association records in church minute books, using
A2A for those already deposited and identified in Record Offices,
references in secondary sources identified above and the Angus
Library. N.B. There will be many not yet listed online.

5. For a study of the **development of the theology and practice**
regarding strict communion or open/closed membership of any
Association make a comparison of the initial statement of faith at the
start of the circular letter or report and significant discussions in the
Minutes at different dates. Compare dates of changes with any
notable statistical changes in membership. Note moves of churches
from one Association to another and see if they correspond with
changes in theology or communion and/or membership practice.
Compare Associations with each other, especially where jurisdictions
overlapped.

N.B. This sample strategy only deals with the English Associations,
but the additional complications of the situation in Wales, where
language as well as theology and practice was a determining factor
cannot be totally ignored owing to cross border links, such as English
churches in North Wales in membership with the Lancashire and
Cheshire Association and some Shropshire churches moving back and
forth between the Shropshire Association and some Welsh
Associations. The Associations in Wales formed three groups: those
only affiliated to the Baptist Union of Great Britain (and Ireland),
those English language Associations in the Baptist Union of Wales
and the Welsh language Associations in the Baptist Union of Wales.

6. Identify the names of any **significant individuals** from any of the
above and look up their biographies and writings to identify
influences on an Association's changing theology.

Check *ODNB; Baptist Handbook* obituaries (indexed on BHS website); bibliographic databases, Starr (online and printed), Whitley and Angus Library catalogue.

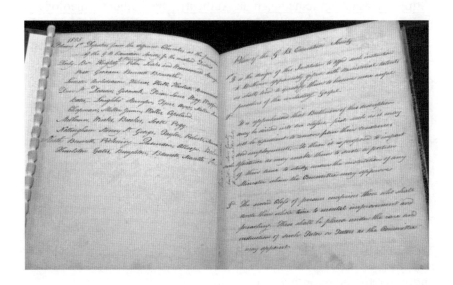

(General Baptist Education Society minutes, 1825-1861: February 1st 1825. RPC)

BAPTIST WEBSITES MENTIONED IN THE TEXT
(HOMEPAGES ONLY)

http://www.abhsarchives.org/

http://www.authenticmedia.co.uk/AuthenticSite/Authentic/theology_
monographs_studies%20in%20baptist%20history%20and%20thought
/page/2

http://www.baptist.org.uk/

http://www.baptistheritage.com

http://www.baptisthistory.org.uk

http://www.baptisthistory.org/

http://www.baptistireland.org/

http://www.baptistsinireland.org/

http://baptistlibraryonline.com

http://www.baptisttheology.org/

http://www.bmsworldmission.org/

http://www.bristol-baptist.ac.uk/

http://www.buw.org.uk/

http://www.bwa-baptist-heritage.org/

http://www.centerforbaptiststudies.org/

http://www.centralba.org.uk/

http://www.exlibris.org/nonconform/engdis/baptists.html

http://www.geocities.com/baptist_documents/index.html

http://www.ibts.eu/

http://www.irishbaptistcollege.co.uk/

http://website.lineone.net/~gsward/noncon.html

http://www.mupress.org/webpages/books/baptistseries.html

http://northernbc.wordpress.com/

http://www.northwalesbaptistcollege.org.uk/welcome.htm

http://www.online-bible.com/baptisthistory.html

http://www.pbfund.org.uk/history.html

http://www.pbpress.org/

http://www.rpc.ox.ac.uk

http://www.sbhla.org/

http://www.scottishbaptist.org.uk/

http://www.scottishbaptistcollege.org/

http://www.shropshirebaptist.org.uk/

http://www.siteone.com/religion/baptist/baptistpage/main.html

http://www.spurgeons.ac.uk/

http://www.spurgeon.org/

http://www.standardbearer.org/

http://www.strictbaptisthistory.org.uk

http://www.swbc.org.uk/

http://www.vor.org/

http://www.wmcarey.edu/carey/

http://www.yellowstone.net/baptist/history.htm

REFERENCES and BIBLIOGRAPHY

2(b) General printed bibliographical sources

[1] Mills, S.J., Sources for the study of Baptist history, *Baptist Quarterly*, xxxiv (6), April 1992, p.282-296.

[2] Devine, J and Egger-Sider, F. *Going beyond Google: the invisible web in learning and teaching*. London: Facet Publishing, 2009.

[3] See http://www3.open.ac.uk/courses/bin/p12.dll?C01TU120

[4] http://www.intute.ac.uk/about.html

[5] http://www.vts.intute.ac.uk/detective/brief.html

[6] Hall, C. *Civilising subjects: metropole and colony in the English imagination, 1830-1867*. Oxford: Polity Press, 2002. Editorial review by John Briggs in *Baptist Quarterly*, 40(3), July 2003, p. 130-132. Also reviewed by H. Temperley in *English Historical Review* 120 (485), p. 158-160, by J.K. Walton in *Journal of Social History* 37(2), 2003, p. 507-509, by E. Said in the *London Review of Books*, 25(6), 20 March 2003,, p. 3,5-6 and in at least 20 other journals.

[7] Oddie, G. A. *Imagined Hinduism: British Protestant missionary constructions of Hinduism, 1793-1900*. New Delhi, London: Sage Publications, 2006. Reviewed by Brian Stanley in *Baptist Quarterly* 42 (4), Oct. 2007, p. 315-317, by H.L. Richard in *International Bulletin of Missionary Research* 31(4), Oct. 2007, p. 213-214 and Paul Hedges in the *Journal of Religious History* 32(1), March 2008, p. 137-138 and at least 5 other journals.

[8] http://www.mundus.ac.uk/ homepage.

[9] Pollard, A.W. & Redgrave, G.R. *A short-title catalogue of books printed in England, Scotland, & Ireland and of English books printed abroad 1475-1640*. 2nd ed. revised & enlarged, begun by W.A. Jackson & F.S. Ferguson; completed by Katharine F. Pantzer. 3 v. London: The Bibliographical Society, 1986-91.

[10] Wing, D.G. *Short-title catalogue of books printed in England, Scotland, Ireland, Wales and British America, and of English books printed in other countries, 1641-1700*. 3 v. New York, 1945-51. 2nd ed. revised and enlarged. 4 v. New York: Modern Language Association of America, 1982-1998.

[11] Wright, C.T. Hagberg. *Subject-index of the London Library*. Vol.1. London: Williams & Norgate, 1909. Vols.2-4, London Library. Additions, 1909-22,1923-38,1938-53. London, 1923, 1938, 1955.

3. Online and printed sources for dissenting history

[12] http://www.exlibris.org/nonconform/engdis/index.html

[13] http://www.intute.ac.uk/artsandhumanities/cgi-bin/fullrecord.pl?handle=20070518-120759

[14] http://www.intute.ac.uk/cgi-bin/search.pl?term1=religious+dissenters+history&limit=0&subject=artsandhumanities&submit.x=12&submit.y=10

[15] http://www.victorianweb.org/religion/dissntrs.html

[16] http://puritanism.online.fr/primary_sources.html

[17] http://www.dwlib.co.uk/dwlib/index.html

[18] Dr Williams's Library. *Catalogue of the Library in Red Cross Street, Cripplegate, founded pursuant to the will of Daniel Williams, who died in the year 1716.* 2 v. London: Richard & John E. Taylor, 1841. Vol. 3 with two supplements: Appendix to the catalogue [Compiled by Richard Cogan]. London: Woodfall & Kinder, 1854. Books, pamphlets, etc., placed in the Library from 1842 to 1885. London, 1885. Catalogue of accessions, 1900-1950: being a catalogue of books published and added to the Library during that period; edited for the Trustees by Doris M. Johnson. London: Dr Williams's Trust, 1955. Catalogue of accessions, vols. 2-4, 1951-1960, 1961-1970, 1971-1980. London: Dr Williams's Trust, 1961, 1972, 1983.

[19] *Early nonconformity, 1566-1800: a catalogue of books in Dr Williams's Library, London.* Author catalogue. Subject catalogue. Chronological catalogue. 12 v. Boston: G. K. Hall, 1968. Photographed card catalogue of the Library's holdings of English Nonconformist books printed 1566-1800.. Known as "Bibliography of Early Nonconformity". Compiled by Miss G. Woodward and Roger Thomas.

[20] Field, C.D. Preserving Zion: the anatomy of Protestant Nonconformist archives in Great Britain and Ireland. *Archives,* xxxiii(118), April 2008, pp. 14-51.

[21] Mullett, M. *Sources for the history of English nonconformity 1660-1830.* [London]: British Records Association, 1991. (Archives and the user, no. 8.) ISBN: 0900222093

[22] Nuttall, G.F. *Studies in English dissent.* Weston Rhyn, Shropshire: Quinta Press, 2002. ISBN: 1897856148

[23] Watts, M.R. *The dissenters.* Oxford: Clarendon Press, c1978-95. 2 v. Vol. 1. From the Reformation to the French Revolution. -- Vol. 2. The expansion of evangelical nonconformity (1995). ISBN: 0198224605 (v.1) 0198229682 (v.2)

[24] Johnson, D.A. *The changing shape of English nonconformity, 1825-1925*. New York, Oxford: Oxford University Press, 1999.

[25] Briggs, J.H.Y. Editorial review of Johnson, D.A. *The changing shape of English nonconformity, 1825-1925* in *Baptist Quarterly* 40(6), April 2004, p. 322-325.

[26] Cornwall, R.D. Review of Johnson, D.A. *The changing shape of English nonconformity, 1825-1925* in *Church history* 69(1) March 2000, p. 210-211.

[27] Brown, K.D. *A social history of the nonconformist ministry in England and Wales, 1800-1930*. Oxford: Clarendon Press, 1988.

[28] Lovegrove, D.W. *Established church, sectarian people: itinerancy and the transformation of English dissent, 1780-1830*. Cambridge: Cambridge University Press, 1988.

[29] Hopkins, M. *Nonconformity's romantic generation: evangelical and liberal theologies in Victorian England*. Milton Keynes: Paternoster, 2004. (Studies in Evangelical history and thought) Reviewed by Christine Lumsden in *Baptist Quarterly* 42(2), April 2007, p. 181.

[30] Bebbington, D.W. *Evangelicalism in modern Britain: a history from the 1730s to the 1980s*. London: Routledge, 1993 (previously published by Unwin Hyman in 1989).

[31] Noll, M.A. *The rise of evangelicalism: the age of Edwards, Whitefield and the Wesleys*. Nottingham: Inter-Varsity Press, 2004.

[32] Sell, A.P.F. and Cross, A.R. (eds.) *Protestant nonconformity in the twentieth century*. Carlisle: Paternoster, 2003. Reviewed by Ian Randall in *Baptist Quarterly* 40(8), Oct. 2004, p. 510-511.

[33] Sell, A.P.F. *Nonconformist theology in the twentieth century*. Carlisle: Paternoster Press, 2006. Reviewed by Keith Clements in *Baptist Quarterly* 42(4), October 2007, p. 319.

[34]http://www.authenticmedia.co.uk/AuthenticSite/category/theology_monographs_studies+in+evangelical+history+and+thought/
http://www.authenticmedia.co.uk/AuthenticSite/Authentic/theology_monographs_studies%20in%20christian%20history%20and%20thought/page/1 and
http://www.authenticmedia.co.uk/AuthenticSite/category/theology_monographs_paternoster+theological+monographs/

4. Secondary sources specific to Baptist history

4(a) Electronic

[35] *The concise Oxford dictionary of the Christian church*; [edited by] E.A. Livingstone. Rev. 2nd ed. Oxford: Oxford University Press, 2006.

[36] *The Oxford companion to British history*; edited by John Cannon. Rev. ed. Oxford: Oxford University Press, 2002.

[37] A *dictionary of British History*; edited by John Cannon. Oxford: Oxford University Press, 2004.

[38] http://www.baptistheritage.com/whoarewe.htm

[39] Gourley, B. "A very brief introduction to Baptist, history then and now" http://www.yellowstone.net/baptist/history.htm

[40] http://www.yellowstone.net/baptist/history.htm

[41] Kreitzer, L.J. '1653 or 1656: when did Oxford Baptists join the Abingdon Association', in Thompson, P.E. and Cross, A.R. (eds.): *Recycling the past or researching history?: studies in Baptist historiography and myths*. Milton Keynes: Paternoster, 2005, p. 207-219.

4(b)(i) Bibliographies

[42] Whitley, W.T. *A Baptist bibliography: being a register of the chief materials for Baptist history, whether in manuscript or in print, preserved in Great Britain, Ireland and the Colonies [1526-1837]*. 2 v. London: Kingsgate Press, 1916-1922. Reprint, 2 v. in 1. Hildesheim, New York: G. Olms, 1984. ISBN: 3487074567.

[43] Starr, E.C. *A Baptist bibliography. being a register of printed material by and about Baptists; including works written against the Baptists*. 25 v. Philadelphia: Judson Press for the Samuel Colgate Baptist Historical Collection, Colgate University, 1947-76. (Vols. 2-4 have imprint: Chester, Pa., American Baptist Historical Society; vols. 5-25 have imprint: Rochester, N.Y., American Baptist Historical Society).

[44] McIntyre, W.E. *Baptist authors: a manual of bibliography, 1500-1914*. [Number 1(-3); A(-Day)] 3 pts. in 1 v. Montreal, Toronto: Industrial and Educational Press, [1914].

[45] *Baptists in Canada 1760-1990: a bibliography of selected printed resources in English*; prepared by Philip G A Griffin-Allwood, George A Rawlyk, Jarold K. Zeman. Hantsport, N.S.: Lancelot Press; Acadia Divinity College; Baptist Historical Committee of United Baptist Convention of the Atlantic Provinces, 1989.

[46] *Nonconformist congregations in Great Britain: a list of histories and other material in Dr Williams's Library*. London: Dr Williams's Trust, 1973.

[47] *A bibliography of Baptist writings on Baptism, 1900-1968*; compiled by Athol Gill. Rüschlikon-Zürich: Baptist Theological Seminary, 1969.

[48] Kingdon, D.P. *Bibliography of books on Baptist history*. [Belfast: the author, c1970]

[49] Shepherd, P. *The making of a modern denomination: John Howard Shakespeare and the English Baptists 1894-1924*. Carlisle: Paternoster, 2001. Reviewed by Keith G. Jones in *Journal of European Baptist Studies* 3(3), May 2003, p. 38-40.

4(b)(ii) Printed Baptist histories

[50] Baptist Union of Great Britain [and Ireland]. *The Baptist Union Directory for ...* London, Didcot: Published annually under the direction of the Council of the Baptist Union of Great Britain [and Ireland], 1973- . [From 1988 Baptist Union of Great Britain].

[51] Hayden, R. *English Baptist history and heritage*. 2nd ed. Didcot: Baptist Union of Great Britain, 2005. Editorial review by J.H.Y. Briggs in *Baptist Quarterly* 41(3), July 2005, p. 130-133.

[52] White, B.R. *The English Baptists of the seventeenth century*. Rev. and expanded ed. Didcot: Baptist Historical Society, c1996.

[53] Brown, R. *The English Baptists of the eighteenth century*. London: Baptist Historical Society, c1986.

[54] Briggs, J.H.Y. *The English Baptists of the nineteenth century*. Didcot: Baptist Historical Society, c1994.

[55] Randall, I.M. *The English Baptists of the twentieth century*. Didcot: Baptist Historical Society, 2005. Reviewed by David M. Thompson in *Baptist Quarterly* 41(2), April 2005, p.120-122.

[56] Crosby, T. *The history of the English Baptists, from the Reformation to the beginning of the reign of King George I*. 4 v. London: printed for, and sold by, the editor, 1738-1740.

[57] Rippon, J. *The Baptist annual register for 1790 [– 1802], including sketches of the state of religion among different denominations of good men at home and abroad.* 4 v. [London: 1792-1802]

[58] Ivimey, J. *A history of the English Baptists.* 4 v. London: Printed for the author, 1811-30.

[59] Howard, K.W.H. 'Index Nominum Ivimiana'. [unpublished] 1981.

[60] Taylor, A. *The history of the English General Baptists: in two parts.* 2 v. London: Printed for the author, 1818.

[61] Whitley, W.T. *A history of British Baptists.* 2nd rev ed. London: Kingsgate, 1932.

[62] Underwood, A.C. *A history of the English Baptists.* London: Baptist Union Publ. Dept., 1947.

[63] Payne, E.A. *The Baptist Union: a short history.* London: Carey Kingsgate Press, 1959, c1958.

[64] Payne, E.A. *The fellowship of believers: Baptist thought and practice yesterday and today.* Enl. ed. London: Carey Kingsgate Press, 1952.

[65] Payne, E.A. *The Free Church tradition in the life of England.* 3rd ed. rev. London: SCM Press, [1951].

[66] Payne, E.A. *The first generation: early leaders of the Baptist Missionary Society in England and India.* London: Carey Press, [1936?].

[67] Payne, E.A. *The great succession: leaders of the Baptist Missionary Society during the nineteenth century.* 2nd ed. London: Carey Press, 1946.

[68] White, B.R. op. cit. pp. 164-170.

[69] Wood, J.H. *A condensed history of the General Baptists of the New Connexion, preceded by historical sketches of the early Baptists.* London: Simpkin, Marshall; Leicester: Winks, 1847.

[70] Cramp, J.M. *Baptist history from the foundation of the Christian church to the close of the eighteenth century.* London: Elliot Stock, 1868. 1875 edition has the revised title *Baptist history: from the foundation of the Christian church to the present time* and an introduction by Joseph Angus. Also available online at http://www.reformedreader.org/history/cramp/toc.htm.

[71] Evans, B. *The early English Baptists.* London: J. Heaton & Son, 1862.

[72] Ibid. p. x, xi.

[73] Ibid. p. 201-228, within Chapter VI "The Stuart dynasty. James the First."

[74] Carlile, J.C. *The story of the English Baptists.* London: James Clarke, 1905.

[75] Yuille, G. (ed.) *History of the Baptists in Scotland from pre-Reformation times.* Glasgow: Baptist Union of Scotland, [1926].

[76] Bebbington, D.W. (ed.) *The Baptists in Scotland: a history.* Glasgow: Baptist Union of Scotland, 1988.

[77] Talbot, B.R. *The search for a common identity: the origins of the Baptist Union of Scotland 1800-1870.* Carlisle: Paternoster, 2003. pp. [371]-394. Reviewed by John R. Barclay in *Baptist Quarterly,* 40(8), Oct. 2004, p. 506. Reviewed by Keith G. Jones in *Journal of European Baptist Studies,* 4(3), May 2004, p. 63-64.

[78] Fisher, J.S. *Impelled by faith: a short history of the Baptists in Scotland.* Stirling: Scottish Baptist History Project, 1996.

[79] Bassett, T.M. *The Welsh Baptists.* Swansea: Ilston House, 1977.

[80] Bassett, T.M. The Baptists of Wales and the Baptist Missionary Society = Bedyddwyr Cymru a Chymdeithas Genhadol y Bedyddwyr. Swansea: Ilston Press, 1991.

[81] Morgan, D. D. J. *The development of the Baptist movement in Wales between 1714 and 1815 with particular reference to the evangelical revival.* Thesis (D. Phil.)-- University of Oxford, 1986.

[82] Thomas, J. *A history of the Baptist Association in Wales, from the year 1650, to the year 1790.* London: sold by Messrs. Dilly, Button, and Thomas, London; Brown, James, and Cottle, Bristol; Ogle, Edinburgh; Allein, Dublin, 1795. [Also available electronically.]

[83] Thomas, J. *Hanes y Bedyddwyr, ymhlith y Cymry,: o amser yr Apostolion, hyd y flwyddyn hon: yn ddwy ran ...* Caerfyrddin: Argraphwyd, dros yr awdwr, gan John Ross, MDCCLXXVIII.

[84] Manley, K. *'Redeeming love proclaim': John Rippon and the Baptists.* Carlisle: Paternoster, 2004, p. 197, quoting the *Baptist Annual Register,* I (1790-93), p. ii.

[85] James, J.S. *Hanes y Bedyddwyr yn Nghymru.* 4 v. Caerfyrddin: Seren Cymru, 1896-1907.

[86] *Shankland, T. Shankland ar ddiwygwyr Cymru.* [s.l.: Seren Gomer, 1900-1904.] [Series of 16 articles extracted from "Seren Gomer" and bound together in one volume with the spine title "Shankland ar ddiwygwyr Cymru". The first few are a review of Beriah Gwynfe Evans' book, "Diwygwyr Cymru", and the later articles contain general history.]

[87] Thompson, J. *Baptists in Ireland, 1792-1922: a dimension of Protestant dissent.* Thesis (D. Phil.)—University of Oxford, 1988.

[88] Thompson, J. *Century of grace: the Baptist Union of Ireland; a short history, 1895-1995.* Belfast: Baptist Union of Ireland, 1995.

[89] *Irish Baptist Historical Society journal.* Vols. 1-25, 1968/69–1992/3. Belfast: Baptist Union of Ireland, 1969-1993. *Journal of the Irish Baptist Historical Society*, (New Series), Vol. 1- , 1993/94- . Moira: Irish Baptist Historical Society, (from 10, 2002/3 Association of Baptist Churches in Ireland) ISSN:0075-0727.

[90] Dix, Kenneth. *Strict and Particular: English Strict and Particular Baptists in the nineteenth century.* Didcot: Baptist Historical Society for the Strict Baptist Historical Society, c2001. Reviewed by Ian Randall in *Baptist Quarterly* 39(7), July 2002, p. 362-363.

[91] Chambers, R.F. et al. *The Strict Baptist chapels of England.* 5 v. London: Strict Baptist Historical Society, 1952-1968. [Unpublished typescripts of later volumes are kept in the Angus library and presumably also in the Strict Baptist Historical Society's library.]

[92] Paul, S.F. *Further history of the Gospel Standard Baptists.* 6 v. [Brighton: the author, vol. 6 Gospel Standard Baptist Trust Ltd.], 1951-1969.

[93] Naylor, P. *Calvinism, Communion and the Baptists: a study of English Calvinistic Baptists from the late 1600s to the early 1800s.* Carlisle: Paternoster Press, 2003.

[94] Naylor, P. *Picking up a pin for the Lord: English Particular Baptists from 1688 to the early nineteenth century.* London: Grace Pubns., 1992.

[95] Oliver, R.W. *History of the English Calvinistic Baptists 1771-1892: from John Gill to C.H. Spurgeon.* Edinburgh: Banner of Truth Trust, 2006.

[96] Roberts, R.P. *Continuity and change: London Calvinistic Baptists and the Evangelical Revival, 1760-1820.* Wheaton, Ill.: Richard Owen Roberts, c1989.

[97] Wright, S. *The early English Baptists, 1603-1649.* Woodbridge: Boydell Press, 2006. Reviewed by Stephen Copson in *Baptist Quarterly*, 41(6), April 2006, p. 371-373. American review by Jason G. Duesing on http://www.baptisttheology.org/TheEarlyEnglishBaptists.cfm .

[98] *Baptist Quarterly*, 41(6), April 2006, p. 373.

[99] Bell, M.R. *Apocalypse how?: Baptist movements during the English Revolution.* Macon, Ga.: Mercer University Press, c2000.

[100] Copeland, D.A. *Benjamin Keach and the development of Baptist traditions in seventeenth-century England.* Lewiston, N.Y.; Lampeter: Edwin Mellen Press, c2001.

[101] Torbet, R.G. *A history of the Baptists.* Philadelphia: Judson Press, 1950. Rev. 1st British ed. London: Carey Kingsgate Press, 1966. 3rd ed. Valley Forge: Judson Press, 1963, 1975.

[102] McLoughlin, W.G. *New England Dissent, 1630-1833: the Baptists and the separation of church and state.* 2 v. Cambridge, Mass.: Harvard University Press, 1971.

[103] McLoughlin, W.G. *Soul liberty: the Baptists' struggle in New England, 1630-1833.* Hanover, London: University Press of New England for Brown University Press, c1991.

[104] McBeth, H.L. *The Baptist heritage.* Nashville, Tenn.: Broadman Press, c1987.

[105] Brackney, W.H. *The Baptists.* New York: Greenwood, 1988. (Denominations in America, no. 2.)

[106] Brackney, W.H. *Christian voluntarism in Britain and North America: a bibliography and critical assessment.* Westport, Conn.: Greenwood Press, 1995. (Bibliographies and indexes in religious studies, 35).

[107] Brackney, W.H. *Historical dictionary of the Baptists.* Lanham, Md. : Scarecrow Press, 1999. (Historical dictionaries of religions, philosophies, and movements ;no. 25.) Editorial review by J.H.Y. Briggs in *Baptist Quarterly* 38(8), Oct. 2000, p. [365]-366.

[108] Brackney, W.H. *Baptists in North America: an historical perspective.* Oxford: Blackwell, 2006. Editorial review in *Baptist Quarterly*, 41(8), Oct. 2006, p. 450-454.

[109] Brackney, W.H. *A genetic history of Baptist thought: with special reference to Baptists in Britain and North America.* Macon, GA: Mercer University Press, 2004.

[110] Leonard, Bill J. *Baptist ways: a history.* Valley Forge, PA: Judson Press, 2003. Reviewed by J.H.Y. Briggs in *Journal of European Baptist Studies* 4(2), Jan. 2004, p. 56-58. Review by Jason G. Duesing originally published in *Southwestern Journal of Theology* 47(1), Fall 2004, p. 86-89 on http://www.baptisttheology.org/baptistways.cfm.

[111] Leonard, Bill J. *Baptists in America.* New York: Columbia University Press, c2005. Editorial review in *Baptist Quarterly*, 41(8), Oct. 2006, p. 450-454.

[112] Durso, P.R. and K.E. *The story of Baptists in the United States.* Brentwood, Tenn.: Baptist History and Heritage Society, 2006. Editorial review in *Baptist Quarterly*, 41(8), Oct. 2006, p. 450-454. Review by Jason G. Duesing originally published in *Southwestern Journal of Theology,* 48(1), Fall 2005, p. 71-72 on http://www.baptisttheology.org/StoryofBaptistsintheUnitedStates.cfm.

[113] Sutton, J. *A Matter of Conviction: A History of Southern Baptist Engagement with the Culture*. Nashville: B&H Publishing, 2008. Review on http://www.baptisttheology.org/AMatterofConviction.cfm.

[114] Wardin, A.W. *The twelve Baptist tribes in the United States: a historical and statistical analysis*. Atlanta, Ga.: Baptist History and Heritage Society; Nashville, Tenn.: Fields Publishing Inc.; 2007. Reviewed by John Briggs in *Baptist Quarterly* 42(6), April 2008, p. 445-6.

[115] Garrett, J.L. *Baptist theology: a four-century study*. Macon, Ga.: Mercer University Press, 2009.

[116] 'Baptist theology surveyed and evaluated'. Editorial review by John Briggs. *Baptist Quarterly*, 42 (1), Jan. 2007, p.2-3.

[117] *Baptist History and Heritage*, 41(1), Winter 2006, p.119-120. Reviewed by Bill J. Leonard.

[118] *American Baptist Quarterly*, 25(2), Summer 2006, p.220-221. Reviewed by Larry L. Greenfield.

[119] [Briggs, J.H.Y.] Editorial: 'Three perspectives on American Baptist history': W.H. Brackney, *Baptists in North America;* P.R. and K.E. Durso, *The story of Baptists in the United States;* Bill J. Leonard, *Baptists in America*, in *Baptist Quarterly*, 41(8), Oct. 2006, p. 450-454.

[120] Ibid., p. 451.

[121] ATLA (American Theological Library Association) Religion database (institutional subscription required): "Supports religious and theological scholarship in graduate education and faculty research. Contains thousands of citations from international titles and multi-author works in the field of religion. Includes a full range of index citations to journal articles, essays in multi-author works, and book reviews from three ATLA print indexes: Religion Index One (RIO), Religion Index Two (RIT), and Index to Book Reviews in Religion (IBRR). Spans over 50 years with selected records going back to 1818. Coverage 1949 to present, updated quarterly" Accessible by subscription via OCLC/FirstSearch at http://www.oclc.org/home

[122] ATLAS (institutional subscription required). Contains the full text of journal articles and book reviews from international titles and multi-author works in the field of religion. Coverage 1949 to present, updated quarterly.

[123] *Arts & Humanities Citation Index* is a multidisciplinary index covering the journal literature of the arts and humanities. It fully covers 1,144 of the world's leading arts and humanities journals, and it indexes individually selected, relevant items from over 6,800 major science and social science journals. Accessible by subscription via Web of Science http://www.isinet.com/

[124] *British Humanities Index*, searchable online through CSA Illumina in libraries with a subscription. Print version published quarterly: London: Library Association, 1962-; Bowker-Saur, <1990>-1999; Bowker, 2000.

[125] Corrado, S. and Pilli, T. (eds.) *Eastern European Baptist history: new perspectives.* Praha: International Baptist Theological Seminary of the European Baptist Federation, 2007. ISBN: 80-87006-02-X

[126] Andronoviene, L. *Involuntarily free or voluntarily bound: singleness in the Baptistic communities of post-communist Europe.* Praha: International Baptist Theological Seminary of the European Baptist Federation, 2003.

[127] Penner, P.F. (ed.) *Ethnic churches in Europe: a Baptist response.* Schwarzenfeld: Neufeld, 2006. ISBN: 3-937896-42-2

[128] Grams, R.G. and Parushev, P.R. (eds.) *Towards an understanding of European Baptist identity: listening to the Churches in Armenia, Bulgaria, Central Asia, Moldova, North Caucasus, Omsk and Poland; mapping Baptistic identity.* Praha: International Baptist Theological Seminary of the European Baptist Federation, 2006. ISBN: 80-87006-01-1

[129] Jones, K.G. and Randall, I.M. (eds.) *Counter-cultural communities: Baptistic life in twentieth-century Europe.* Milton Keynes: Paternoster, 2008. (Studies in Baptist History and Thought, v. 32.)

[130] Bebbington,D.W. (ed.) *The Gospel in the world: international Baptist studies.* Carlisle: Paternoster, 2002. (Studies in Baptist History and Thought, v.1.) (ICOBS 1) Reviewed by Keith G. Jones in *Journal of European Baptist Studies*, 3(2), Jan. 2003, p.51-2.

[131] Randall, I.M., Pilli, T. and Cross, A.R. (eds.) *Baptist identities: international studies from the seventeenth to the twentieth century.* Milton Keynes: Paternoster, 2006. (Studies in Baptist history and thought, v. 19.) (ICOBS 3)

[132] Randall, I.M. and Cross, A.R. (eds.) *Baptists and mission: papers from the Fourth International Conference on Baptist Studies.* Milton Keynes: Paternoster, 2007. (Studies in Baptist history and thought, v. 29.) (ICOBS 4) Reviewed in *Journal of European Baptist Studies* 9(1), September 2008, p. 51-2.

[133] Adams, F. The people called Ghanaian Baptists. *Baptist Quarterly,* 42(7), July 2008, p. 501-508.

[134] Wardin, A.W. The Baptists in Bulgaria. *Baptist Quarterly*, 34(4), Oct. 1991, p. 148-159.

[135] Pilli, T. Baptists in Estonia, 1884-1940. *Baptist Quarterly*, 39(1), Jan. 2001, p. 27-33.

[136] Pilli, T. From a thunderstorm to a settled still life: Estonian Baptists 1959-1972. *Baptist Quarterly,* 41(4), Oct. 2005, p. 206-223.

[137] Wardin, A.W. Baptist growth in Congress Poland. *Baptist Quarterly,* 39(6), April 2002, p. 298-304.

[138] Davies, R.E. Persecution and growth: a hundred years of Baptist life in Romania. *Baptist Quarterly*, 33(6), April 1990, p. 265-274.

[139] Brandsma, J.A. Johannes Elias Feisser and the rise of the Netherlands Baptists. *Baptist Quarterly*, 16(1), Jan. 1955, p. 10-21.

[140] Rushbrooke, J.H. *The Baptist movement in the continent of Europe.* Rev.ed. London: Carey Press, 1923.

[141] Green, B. *Tomorrow's man: a biography of James Henry Rushbrooke.* Didcot: Baptist Historical Society, c1997.

[142] Green, B. *Crossing the boundaries: a history of the European Baptist Federation.* Didcot: Baptist Historical Society, 1999. Editorial review by John Briggs in *Baptist Quarterly* 38(6), April 2000, p. 261-263.

[143] Green, B. *European Baptists and the Third Reich.* (Forthcoming). Baptist Historical Society, 2009.

[144] Fath, S. *Les Baptistes en France (1810-1950): faits, dates et documents.* Cléon d'Andran: Excelsis, 2002.

[145] Balders, G. (ed.) *Ein Herr, ein Glaube, eine Taufe: 150 Jahre Baptistengemeinden in Deutschland, 1834-1984.* Festschrift im Auftrag des Bundes Evangelisch-Freikirchlicher Gemeinden in Deutschland, unter Mitarbeit von Manfred Bärenfänger ... [et al.]. 2nd ed. Wuppertal: Oncken, 1985.

[146] Strübind, A. *Die unfreie Freikirche: der Bund der Baptistengemeinden im "Dritten Reich".* Neukirchen-Vluyn: Neukirchener, c1991.

[147] Coleman, H.J. *Russian Baptists and spiritual revolution, 1905-1929.* Bloomington, Ind.: Indiana University Press, 2005.

[148] Maselli, D. *Storia dei Battisti italiani: 1873-1923.* Torino: Claudiana, 2003.

[149] [Briggs, J.H.Y.] 'Challenging both tsars and soviets: Russian Baptists 1905-1929', in *Baptist Quarterly* 41(6), April 2006, p.322-325.

[150] Ibid., p. 322.

[151] Ibid., p. 324.

[152] Randall, I. *Communities of conviction: Baptist beginnings in Europe.* [Prague: European Baptist Federation, Projected date May 2009].

[153] Wardin, A.W. (ed.) *Baptists around the world: a comprehensive handbook.* Nashville, TN: Broadman & Holman, 1995.

[154] *The Baptist World Congress: London, July 11-19, 1905; authorized record of proceedings with introduction by J.H. Shakespeare.* London: Baptist Union Publication Department, 1905.

Baptist World Alliance: first European Congress held in Berlin, 1908: authorized record of proceedings with introduction by J.H. Rushbrooke; assistant editor, E.C. Pike. London: Baptist Union Publication Department, 1908.

The Baptist World Alliance: second congress, Philadelphia, June 19-25, 1911; record of proceedings. Philadelphia, PA: printed by Harper & Brother for the Philadelphia Committee, 1911.

Third Baptist World Congress: Stockholm, July 21-27, 1923; record of proceedings edited by W.T. Whitley ; with introduction by J.H. Shakespeare. London : Kingsgate Press, 1923.

Fourth Baptist World Congress: Toronto, Canada, 23-29 June 1928; record of proceedings edited by W.T. Whitley ; with foreword J.H. Rushbrooke. Toronto: Stewart Printing Service; London: Kingsgate Press, [1928].

Fifth Baptist World Congress: Berlin, August 4-10, 1934; official report edited with a foreword J.H. Rushbrooke. London : Baptist World Alliance, 1934.

Sixth Baptist World Congress: Atlanta, Georgia, USA, July 22-28, 1939; official report edited with a foreword by J.H. Rushbrooke. Atlanta, GA: Baptist World Alliance, 1939.

Seventh Baptist World Congress: Copenhagen, Denmark, July 29-August 3, 1947; official report edited by Walter O. Lewis. London : Baptist World Alliance, 1948.

Eighth Baptist World Congress, Cleveland, Ohio, U. S. A. July 22-27, 1950; official report edited by Arnold T. Ohrn. London : Baptist World Alliance, [1950].

Baptist World Alliance Golden Jubilee Congress (ninth world congress), London, England, 16th-22nd July 1955: official report; edited by Arnold T. Ohrn; assisted by Geoffrey W. Rusling. London : Published with the authority of the Baptist

World Alliance by the Carey Kingsgate Press Limited, [1955].

Baptist World Alliance: tenth Baptist World Congress, Rio de Janeiro, Brazil, June 26-July 3, 1960; official report edited by Arnold T. Ohrn; assisted by C.E. Bryant and Hubert Porter. Nashville, TN: Baptist World Alliance, 1961.

The truth that makes men free: official report of the Eleventh Congress, Baptist World Alliance, Miami Beach, Florida, U.S.A., June 25-30, 1965; edited by Josef Nordenhaug ... Nashville, Tenn.: Broadman Press for the Alliance, c1966.)

Reconciliation through Christ: official report of the twelfth congress, Tokyo, Japan, July 12-18, 1970; Robert S. Denny, General Secretary; edited by Cyril E. Bryant. Valley Forge, Pa. : Judson Press, c1971.

New people for a new world - through Christ: official report of the thirteenth congress, Baptist World Alliance, Stockholm, Sweden, July 8-13, 1975. Robert S. Denny, General Secretary; edited by Cyril E. Bryant and Debbie Stewart. Nashville, Tenn. : Published for the Baptist World Alliance by Broadman Press, c1976.

Celebrating Christ's presence through the Spirit: official report of the Fourteenth Congress, Baptist World Alliance, Toronto, Canada, July 8-13, 1980. Robert S. Denny, general secretary; edited by Cyril E. Bryant and Ruby J. Burke. Nashville, Tenn.: Broadman Press for the Baptist World Alliance, c1981.

Out of darkness into the Light of Christ: official report of the fifteenth Congress, Baptist World Congress, Los Angeles, California, July 2-7, 1985. [Nashville, Tenn.?]: Published for the Baptist World Alliance, 1985.

Together in Christ: official report of the sixteenth congress: Baptist World Congress, Seoul, Korea August 14-19, 1990; edited by Wendy E. Ryan. McLean, VA : Baptist World Alliance, [1990].

Come celebrate Christ: the hope of the world. Baptist World Congress (17th : 1995: Buenos Aires, Argentina.) [McLean, Va.?]: Baptist World Alliance, 1995.

"Jesus Christ forever. Yes!": 18th Baptist World Congress January 5-9, 2000 Melbourne, Australia. McLean, VA : Baptist World Alliance, c2000.

Official report of the Centenary Baptist World Congress: Birmingham, England, July 27-31, 2005. Falls Church, Va.: Baptist World Alliance, c2006.

[155] *Baptists together in Christ, 1905-2005: a hundred-year history of the Baptist World Alliance.* Richard V. Pierard, general editor. Falls Church, Va.: Baptist World Alliance, c2005.

[156] Lord, F.T. *Baptist world fellowship: a short history of the Baptist World Alliance.* London: Carey Kingsgate Press, [1955].

[157] Hudson-Reed, S. ed. *Together for a century: the history of the Baptist Union of South Africa, 1877-1977.* Pietermaritzburg: S.A. Baptist Historical Society, [1977].

[158] Atanda, J.A. (ed.) *Baptist churches in Nigeria, 1850-1950: accounts of their foundation and growth.* Ibadan: University Press, 1988.

[159] Tonson, P. *A handful of grain: the centenary history of the Baptist Union of N.Z.* 4 v. Wellington, N.Z.: N.Z. Baptist Historical Society for the Baptist Union of New Zealand, [1982]-1984.

[160] Sutherland, M. (ed.) *Baptists in colonial New Zealand: documents illustrating Baptist life and development.* Auckland: New Zealand Baptist Research and Historical Society, 2002. Reviewed by Roger Hayden in *Baptist Quarterly* 40(4), Oct. 2003, p. 254-255.

[161] Manley, K.R. *From Woolloomooloo to 'eternity': a history of Australian Baptists.* 2 v. Milton Keynes: Paternoster, 2006. (Studies in Baptist history and thought, v. 16.) Reviewed by Roger Hayden in *Baptist Quarterly* 42(8),Oct. 2008, p. 613-616. Reviewed by I.M. Randall in *Journal of European Baptist Studies*, 7(2), Jan. 2007, p. 50-51.

[162] Brackney, W.H., Fiddes, P.S. and Briggs, J.H.Y. (eds.) *Pilgrim pathways: essays in Baptist history in honour of B.R. White.* Macon, Ga.: Mercer University Press, c1999. Reviewed by Kenneth B.E. Roxburgh in *Baptist Quarterly* 39(1), Jan. 2001, p. 44. American review by Jason K. Lee on http://www.baptisttheology.org/PilgrimPathways.cfm

[163] Thompson, P.E. and Cross, A.R. (eds.): *Recycling the past or researching history?: studies in Baptist historiography and myths.* Milton Keynes: Paternoster, 2005. (Studies in Baptist history and thought, v. 11.)

[164] Ibid. p. xiii-xiv.

4(b)(iii) English Association and regional histories

[165] Buffard, F. *Kent and Sussex Baptist Associations.* Faversham: E. Vinson, [1964].

[166] Elwyn, T.H.S. *The Northamptonshire Baptist Association*. London: Carey Kingsgate Press, 1964.

[167] Johnson, C.J. *Encounter in London: the story of the London Baptist Association, 1865-1965*. London: Carey Kingsgate Press, 1965.

[168] West Midlands Baptist Association. *Records of an old association: being a memorial volume of the 250th anniversary of the Midland, now the West Midland, Baptist Association, formed in Warwick, May 3rd, 1655*; [edited by J.M. Gwynne Owen]. [Birmingham: Allday, 1905.]

[169] Harrison, F.M.W. *It all began here: the story of the East Midland Baptist Association*. London: East Midlands Baptist Association, c1986.

[170] Langley, A.S. *Birmingham Baptists, past and present: prepared for the West Midland Baptist Association*. London: Kingsgate Press, [1939].

[171] Klaiber, A.J. *The story of the Suffolk Baptists*. London: Kingsgate Press, [1931]

[172] Payne, E.A. *The Baptists of Berkshire through three centuries*. London: Carey Kingsgate Press, [1951].

[173] Witard, D. *Bibles in barrels: a history of Essex Baptists*. [Colchester]: Essex Baptist Association, [1962].

[174] Browne, J. *History of Congregationalism and memorials of the churches in Norfolk and Suffolk*. London: Jarrold and Sons, 1877.

[175] Greasley, S. *The Baptists of Derbyshire: 1650-1914*. Ilkeston: Moorley's Print & publishing, c2007. Reviewed by Peter Shepherd in *Baptist Quarterly*, 42(8), October 2008, p. 628-630.

[176] Collis, M.J. *Shropshire Baptist history: an account of the Baptist churches of Shropshire and surrounding areas*. [Shrewsbury?]: Shropshire Group of Baptist Churches, 2008. ISBN 978-0-9560329-0-4 Details and excerpts at http://www.shropshirebaptist.org.uk/book.htm

[177] Whitley, W.T. *Baptists of North-West England: 1649-1913*. London, Preston: Kingsgate, Toulmin, for the Lancashire & Cheshire Association, 1913.

[178] *The Baptists of Yorkshire: being the centenary memorial volume of the Yorkshire Baptist Association*. Bradford, London: Byles, Kingsgate, 1912. (An augmented edition of these 2 titles was published in 1913, see below.)

[179] *Baptists in Yorkshire, Lancashire, Cheshire & Cumberland*. London: Kingsgate Press [for the Baptist Historical Society], 1913. (spine title: *Baptists in Yorkshire and the North-west*).

[180] Copson, S.L. *Association life of the Particular Baptists of Northern England 1699-1732.* [London]: Baptist Historical Society, 1991. (English Baptist Records, 3)

[181] Douglas, D. *History of the Baptist churches in the North of England: from 1648 to 1845.* London: Houlston and Stoneman, 1846.

[182] Neil, D.F. *The Baptists of North East England 1650-2000.* Houghton-le-Spring: the author, 2006.

[183] Murch, J. *A history of the Presbyterian and General Baptist churches in the West of England: with memoirs of some of their pastors.* London: Hunter, 1835.

[184] Doel, W. *Twenty golden candlesticks: or a history of Baptist nonconformity in western Wiltshire.* Trowbridge: B. Lansdown and Sons and George Rose; London: Simpkin, Marshall, Hamilton, Kent & Co., 1890. Facsimile reprint published 2005, obtainable from Wiltshire County Council see http://eshop.wiltshire.gov.uk/getshopitem.php?id=8.

[185] Briggs, J.H.Y. Review of William Doel: *Twenty golden candlesticks: or a history of Baptist nonconformity in western Wiltshire* (2005 facsimile reprint) in *Baptist Quarterly* 41(5), Jan. 2006, p. 319-320.

[186] Jones, A.D. *Twenty golden candlesticks revisited: Wiltshire Baptist history 1890-2005.* Published by the author, 2008.

[187] Review of the above by John Briggs in *Baptist Quarterly,* 43(1), Jan. 2009, p. 34.

4(b)(iv) Local church histories

[188] Dr Williams's Library. *Nonconformist congregations in Great Britain: a list of histories and other material in Dr Williams's Library.* London : Dr Williams's Trust, 1973.

[189] Stell, C. *An inventory of nonconformist chapels and meeting-houses in central England.* London: H.M.S.O., 1986. Royal Commission on the Historical Monuments of England.

[190] Stell, C. *An inventory of nonconformist chapels and meeting-houses in south-west England.* London: H.M.S.O., 1991. Royal Commission on Historical Monuments (England).

[191] Stell, C. *An inventory of nonconformist chapels and meeting-houses in the north of England.* London: H.M.S.O., 1994. Royal Commission on Historical Monuments (England).

[192] Stell, C. *An inventory of nonconformist chapels and meeting-houses in Eastern England.* Swindon: English Heritage, 2002. Editorial review by John Briggs in *Baptist Quarterly* 40(1), Jan. 2003, p. 2-5.

[193] Kreitzer, L.J. *'Seditious Sectaryes': the Baptist Conventiclers of Oxford 1641-1691.* Milton Keynes: Paternoster, 2006. (Studies in Baptist history and thought, v. 30) Reviewed by Stephen Copson on the Baptist Historical Society website: http://www.baptisthistory.org.uk/bhs_articles/reviews/review010.pdf.

[194] Ibid. p. 7.

[195] http://www.baptisthistory.org.uk/bhs_articles/reviews/review010.pdf

[196] Chadwick, R.E. (ed.) *A Protestant Catholic church of Christ: essays on the history and life of New Road Baptist Church, Oxford.* Oxford: New Road Baptist Church, 2003. Reviewed by Stephen Copson in *Baptist Quarterly* 40(6), April 2004, p. 382. Reviewed by Keith G. Jones in *Journal of European Baptist Studies* 4(1), September 2003, p. 39-40.

[197] Binfield, C. *Pastors and people: the biography of a Baptist church, Queen's Road Coventry.* Coventry: Queen's Road Baptist Church, 1984.

[198] Ibid. p. 6.

[199] Bowers, F. *A bold experiment: the story of Bloomsbury Chapel and Bloomsbury Central Baptist Church, 1848-1999.* London: Bloomsbury Central Baptist Church, 1999. Editorial review by John Briggs in *Baptist Quarterly* 38(5), Jan. 2000, p. 209-210.

[200] Mitchell, S. *Not disobedient: a history of United Baptist Church, Leicester, including Harvey Lane 1760-1845, Belvoir Street 1845-1940, and Charles Street 1831-1940. [A brief history of] United Baptist Church 1940-1983; Graham Lee.* [Leicester: S. Mitchell], c1984.

[201] Cramer, S.A. *Loughborough Baptists and the town.* Loughborough Baptist Church, 2000. Short review by J.H.Y. Briggs in *Baptist Quarterly*, 39(2), April 2001, p.79.

[202] Brewer, J. *An outline history of the General Baptists of Loughborough, 1760 to 1975.* Loughborough: the author, 1979.

[203] Cramer, op. cit., p. 2.

[204] Gibbins, H.D. *The history and development of the Baptist churches in Middlesborough.* [Middlesborough?]: the author, 1994. ISBN 0952383101.

[205] Bonsall, H.E. with Robertson, E.H. *The dream of an ideal city: Westbourne Park, 1877-1977.* London: Westbourne Park Baptist Church; York: Sessions, 1978.

[206] Gregory, F. and Willett, P. *Deacon's dissenters raise the cross: the history, origin & memoirs of Cross Hills Baptist Church.* Coalville, Leics.: Catamount, 1998.

[207]Ibid. p. ix.

[208] Godfrey, J.R. *Historic memorials of Barton & Melbourne General Baptist churches: including their numerous offshoots since 1760; biographical sketches of the leading ministers and laymen; together with portraits and other illustrations.* Leicester: Buck, Winks and Son, 1891.

[209] *Memoirs of the late Mr. Samuel Deacon: who was nearly forty years pastor and fifty years a member of the General Baptist Church, Barton, Leicestershire; with extracts from his various writings, letters, &c.* Loughborough: printed and sold at the General Baptist Printing-Office, [1827?]

[210] Hambleton, M.G. *A sweet and hopeful people: the story of Abingdon Baptist Church 1649-2000.* Abingdon: the author, 2000. Reviewed by Michael Collis in *Baptist Quarterly*, 39(4), Oct. 2001, p. 204-5.

[211] Spyvee, H. *Colchester Baptist Church - the first 300 years, 1689-1989: now worshipping at Eld Lane and Blackheath.* Colchester: Colchester Baptist Church, 1989.

[212] Chadwick, R.E. *Sacred ground, high tradition: Salendine Nook Baptist Church 1743-1993.* [s.l.: s.n., 1993]

[213] Stock, J. *History of the Baptised Independent and Congregational Church, meeting in Salendine Nook chapel, Huddersfield.* London: Elliot Stock, [187-].

[214] [Stock, P.] *Foundations: [a history of Salendine Nook Baptist Chapel, Huddersfield].* Halifax: Edward Mortimer, 1933.

[215] Chadwick, R.E. and Joynes, D.W. *'Persistent efforts and untiring labours': Beulah Baptist Church, Hollinwood, Oldham 1891-1991.* [Hollinwood: Printed by the Commercial Centre, 1991?]

[216] Jeal, R. *Maidstone Baptist Church, 1834-1984.* [Maidstone: Maidstone Baptist Church, 1984?]

[217] Jordan, E.K.H. *The church at the Hay Well: how Baptists came to Malvern.* Malvern: Malvern Baptist Church, 1987.

[218] Evans, G.E. *Come wind, come weather: chronicles of Tilehouse Street Baptist Church, 1669-1969.* London, Tonbridge: Whitefriars P., 1969.

[219] Clark, W.P. *Eythorne: our Baptist heritage.* [Sandwich: W. Philip Clark, 1981]

[220] *"As witness this day": Princes Risborough Baptist Church, 1707-2007; a celebration.* [Princes Risborough: Princes Risborough Baptist Church, 2007.]

[221] Fisher, J.S. *People of the Meeting House: tales of a church in Luton.* [Luton?: s.n., 1976?]

[222] Fereday L.A. *The story of Falmouth Baptists: with some account of Cornish Baptist beginnings.* London: Carey Kingsgate Press, [1950].

[223] Overend, F. *History of the Ebenezer Baptist Church, Bacup. Together with an historical account of the "Church of Christ in Rossendale", based on the Mitchel and Crosley letters, hitherto unpublished.* London: Kingsgate Press, 1912.

[224] Nicholson, H.M. *Authentic records relating to the Christian church now meeting in George Street and Mutley Chapels, Plymouth, 1640-1870.* London: Elliot Stock, [1870?].

[225] Price, S.J. *Upton: the story of one hundred and fifty years 1785-1935.* London: Carey Press, 1935.

[226] Hayden, E.W. *A centennial history of Spurgeon's Tabernacle.* London: Clifford Frost, 1962. Reprinted with an additional chapter and bibliographical appendices. Pasadena, Tex: Pilgrim Publications, 1971.

4(b)(v) Periodicals

[227] *Transactions of the Baptist Historical Society*, vols. 1-7, 1908/09 – 1920/21. London: Baptist Union Publication Dept.

[228] *The Baptist quarterly.* vol. 1, no. 1 - , 1922 – . London: Baptist Historical Society. [for index details see http://www.baptisthistory.org.uk]

[229] *Seren Gomer: [neu, Gyfrwng gwybodaeth cyffredinol].* Abertawe [Swansea] : Joseph Harris, 1818-1983. Many different publishers and printers; later places include: Caerfyrddin, Aberdar (1880-1897), Tonypandy (1897-1906), Barmouth, Dinbych, Llandysul (1943-1983). Subtitles vary: None on earliest issues; cyhoeddiad chwarterol (1861-1865); cylchgrawn chwarterol Undeb Bedyddwyr Cymru (1880-1887); cylchgrawn daufisol Undeb Bedyddwyr Cymru (1888-1951); cylchgrawn chwarterol Bedyddwyr Cymru (1952-1974)

[230] *American Baptist Quarterly,* vol. 1, no. 1 - , 1982 –. Rochester, N.Y., American Baptist Historical Society. [Preceded by *Foundations: a Baptist journal of history and theology,* vols. 1-25, 1958-1982 and *The Chronicle: a Baptist historical quarterly,* vols. 1-20, 1938-1957.]

[231] *Baptist history and heritage*, vol. 1- , 1965 - . Nashville, Tenn., Shawnee, Oklahoma (1997-99); Brentwood, Tennessee (1999-2007); Atlanta, Georgia (2007-present).: Historical Commission of the Southern Baptist Convention, Southern Baptist Historical Society, Baptist History & Heritage Society.

[232] *Journal of Ecclesiastical History,* Vol. 1, no. 1 - , Apr. 1950 – . London: Cambridge University Press.

[233] *Church history,* vol. 1 - , Mar. 1932 - . [Chicago, etc.]: American Society of Church History.

[234] *The International Review of Mission(s).* Edinburgh: International review of missions; Geneva: Commission on World Mission and Evangelism of the World Council of Churches., vol. 1 - , 1912 - . From April 1969 entitled *International Review of Mission.* Vols. for Jan. 1912-Oct. 1921 issued by the Continuation Committee of the World Missionary Conference; Jan. 1922-Jan. 1962, by International Missionary Council; Apr. 1962- by the Commission on World Mission and Evangelism of the World Council of Churches. (Available electronically.)

[235] *International Bulletin of Missionary Research.* New Haven: Overseas Missionary Study Center, 1981 - . 1950 -1976 as *Occasional bulletin from the Missionary Research Library*; 1977-1980 as *Occasional bulletin of Missionary Research.* Available electronically.

[236] Ibid. vol. 97, no. 3841385, Jan./Apr. 2008, pp. 161-179.

[237] http://www.oikoumene.org/en/programmes/unity-mission-evangelism-and-spirituality/mission-and-unity/irm.html.

[238] *Journal of European Baptist Studies*, Vol.1, no. 1 - , Sept. 2000 – . Prague: International Baptist Theological Seminary.

[239] Randall, I. *Journal of European Baptist Studies*, 1(1), Sept. 2000, p. 2-3.

[240] *The Baptist Handbook.* London: J. Heaton & Son, Elliot Stock, Yates and Alexander, Veale, Chiffereale & Co., Baptist Union Publication Dept., 1861-1972.

[241] *The Baptist Union Directory*, London: edited and published under the direction of the Council of the Baptist Union of Great Britain (and Ireland), 1973/4 -

[242] Baptist Union of Great Britain and Ireland. *Account of the proceedings of the annual meeting of the ministers and members of the Baptist denomination in London, 1832: with a comparative table of the state of the denomination in 1790 and 1832.* Title varies *Account of the proceedings of the annual meeting of the Baptist Union in London, 1833 [-1834]: with a report of the state of the denomination; Account of the proceedings of the twenty-third [-thirty-second] annual meeting [or session] of the Baptist Union, held in London ... 1835 [-1844]: with a report of the state of the*

denomination. London: 1832-1840 published by Wightman, 1841-1844 published by Houlston and Stoneman . Reports for 1836-1839 each include a folded table of membership levels.

[243] Baptist Union of Great Britain & Ireland. *A manual of the Baptist denomination*. London: Houlston and Stoneman/ Houlston and Wright, 1845-1859.

[244] Rippon, J. *The Baptist Annual Register,* 4 v. Or 41 parts. London, etc.: various booksellers, 1790-1802. (Vol. 1 available electronically*)*

[245] Manley, K. *'Redeeming love proclaim': John Rippon and the Baptists.* Carlisle: Paternoster, 2004. (Studies in Baptist History and Thought, v. 12.) (Reviewed by Peter J. Morden in *Baptist Quarterly,* 41(1), Jan. 2005, p. 61-62. Short review in *Journal of European Baptist Studies,* 5(1), Sept. 2004, p. 64.) Chapter 5: "Wider horizons: *The Baptist Annual Register* (1790-1902)", p. 139-195. The first part of Chapter 6: "Rippon and Baptist historiography", p. 196-205, continues the discussion of "materials of a historical nature published in the *Register".*

[246] *Scottish Baptist Yearbook.* Glasgow: Baptist Union of Scotland, 1925 - . [1925-1968 as *Scottish Baptist year-book for ...*

[247] *Baptist Magazine*, vols. 1-96, London: various publishers, 1809-1904.

[248] 'A list of the Particular Baptist Churches and ministers in England, Corrected to October, 1811'. *Baptist Magazine,* v. 3, 1811, p. 458-463.

[249] 'Intelligence, &c. List of the Particular or Calvinistic Baptist Churches in England.' *Baptist Magazine,* 1823, p. 23-29, 159-162, 331-332, 432-434.

[250] 'List of Particular or Calvinistic Baptist Churches'. *Baptist Magazine,* 1827, p. 32-35, 80-83, 135-139.

[251] 'List of Baptist churches in England for 1831, with the date of their formation, the names of their present ministers, and the year of their settlement'. *Baptist Magazine,* 1831, p. 160-164, 203-207.

[252] 'Statistical account of Evangelical Baptist churches in England'. *Baptist Magazine,* 1835, p. 549-566.

[253] 'A list of the Particular Baptist churches and ministers in Wales'. *Baptist Magazine,* 3, 1811. p. 496-497.

[254] 'List of Baptist churches in Wales for 1831'. *Baptist Magazine,* 1831, p. 499-503.

[255] 'List of Baptist churches in Scotland for 1831'. Ibid., p. 503-504.

[256] *Baptist Magazine,* 1823, p. 23.

[257] Ibid.

[258] 'An alphabetical list of the Baptist ministers in England, with the places where they are settled, the dates of their settlement; and also the period when the church was formed over which they respectively preside; as far as these items have been ascertained, made up nearly to the close of the present year 1831.'. *Baptist Magazine,* 1831, p. 590-597. General Baptist ministers are listed separately, p. 598, and Baptist missionaries, p. 599.

[259] Breed, G.R. *My ancestors were Baptists: how can I find out more about them?* Rev. ed. London: Society of Genealogists, 2007. 4th ed. 2002, p. 17.

[260] *The New Baptist Miscellany, conducted by members of the Baptist denomination..* London: Holdsworth and Ball, 1831, p. 23-32.

[261] *The Sword and the Trowel: a record of combat with sin and labour for the Lord*; edited by C.H. Spurgeon. London: Passmore & Alabaster, 1865 -

4(b)(vi) Biographical sources

[262] Thomson, R.W. *Heroes of the Baptist Church*. London: Kingsgate Press, 1937.

[263] Shakespeare, J.H. *Baptist and Congregational pioneers.* [2nd ed.] London: National Council of Evangelical Free Churches, [1907].

[264] Greaves, R.L. & Zaller, R., (eds.) *Biographical Dictionary of British radicals in the seventeenth century*. 3 vols. Brighton: Harvester Press, 1982-4.

[265] Lewis, D.M., (ed.) *The Blackwell dictionary of evangelical biography: 1730-1860.* Oxford: Blackwell, 1995.

[266] *Biographical dictionary of evangelicals*; ed. T. Larsen; consulting eds., D. Bebbington, M. A. Noll. Leicester: Inter-Varsity Press, 2003. Reviewed by Stephen Copson in *Baptist Quarterly,* 41(3), July 2005, p. 191.

[267] Matthews, A.G. *Calamy revised: being a revision of Edmund Calamy's Account of the ministers and others ejected and silenced 1660-2*. Oxford: Clarendon Press, 1934 (rev. 1988)

[268] Matthews, A.G. *Walker revised, being a revision of John Walker's Sufferings of the clergy during the Grand Rebellion 1642-60*. Oxford: Clarendon Press, 1948 (rev. 1988).

[269] Calamy, E. (rev. Palmer, S.) *The Nonconformist's memorial: being an account of the ministers, who were ejected or silenced after the Restoration, particularly by the Act of Uniformity, ... Aug. 24, 1662. Containing a concise view of their lives and characters*, ... Originally written by ... Edmund Calamy, D.D. Now abridged and corrected and the author's additions inserted, ... by Samuel Palmer. 2nd ed. 2 v. London: printed for W. Harris [and] Alexander Hogg, 1775-8. [Available electronically.]

[270] Neal, D. *The history of the Puritans, or, Protestant non-conformists, ... with an account of their principles...* New ed., revised, corrected, and enlarged by Joshua Toulmin. 5 v. Bath, London, Bristol: 1793-1797. [Available electronically, as well as on the microfilm The Eighteenth Century ; reel 3653, no. 01]

[271] Wilson, W. *The history and antiquities of dissenting churches and meeting houses in London, Westminster and Southwark, including the lives of their ministers.* 4 v. London: Printed for the author; sold by W. Button and Son ...; T. Williams and Son ...; and J. Conder ..., 1808-[1814].

[272] Jones, J.A. (ed.) *Bunhill memorials: sacred reminiscences of three hundred ministers and other persons of note, who are buried in Bunhill Fields, of every denomination* ... London: James Paul, 1849.

[273] Light, A.W. *Bunhill Fields: written in honour and to the memory of the many saints of God whose bodies rest in this old London cemetery.* 2 v. London: Farncombe, 1913, 1933. (Reprinted in one volume in 2003 by Tentmaker Publications.)

[274] Couling, S. *The dead in Christ, or, The Baptists in Bunhill Fields.* London: Baptist Tract Society, [1871?]

[275] Boase, F. *Modern English biography, containing many thousand concise memoirs of persons who have died between the years of 1851-1900: with an index of the most interesting matter.* 6 v. [London]: Cass, 1965. (Reprint of 1st ed., originally published, Netherton & Worth, 1892-1921)

[276] Ibid. p. [iii].

[277] The *dictionary of Welsh biography down to 1940*; [editors: 1943-7 Sir John Edward Lloyd, 1943-59 R.T. Jenkins]. London: Honourable Society of Cymmrodorion, 1959.

[278] *The dictionary of Welsh biography, 1941-1970: together with a supplement to The dictionary of Welsh biography down to 1940*; [The late R. T. Jenkins, the late E. D. Jones, Brynley F. Roberts (editors)]. London: Honourable Society of Cymmrodorion, 2001.

[279] *Dictionary of Scottish biography*; ed. Kenneth Roy. Irvine: Carrick Media, c1999-.

[280] *Chambers Scottish biographical dictionary;* ed. Rosemary Goring. Edinburgh: Chambers, 1992.

[281] Crone, J.S. *A concise dictionary of Irish biography.* Rev. ed. Dublin: Talbot Press, 1937.

[282] Breed, G.R. *My ancestors were Baptists: how can I find out more about them?* Rev. ed. London: Society of Genealogists, 2007. [obtainable from the Society of Genealogists http://www.sog.org.uk/acatalog/My_Ancestors_Series.html or the Strict Baptist Historical Society http://www.strictbaptisthistory.org.uk/publications.htm]

[283] Ruston, A. *My ancestors were English Presbyterians or Unitarians: how can I find out more about them?* 2nd ed. London: Society of Genealogists, 2001.

[284] *The evangelical magazine,* Vols. 1-20, 1793- 1812. London: printed for the editors by T. Chapman; and sold by Chapman & Co., 1793-1812. Later titles: *The evangelical magazine and missionary chronicle* (1813-1883), *The evangelical magazine with which is issued The missionary chronicle* (1884-1890). *The evangelical magazine* (1891-1903), *The evangelical magazine and The British missionary.* 1903 - .

[285] *The gentleman's magazine, or, Monthly intelligencer,* London: 1731-1735; *The gentleman's magazine,* 1736-1914, (with varying titles and imprints).

[286] Ruston, A. *Obituaries and marriages of dissenting ministers in the Gentleman's Magazine in the 18th century,* extracted and annotated by Alan Ruston. Watford: Alan Ruston, 1996.

[287] *The Baptist Times.* Weekly. London, Sept. 10th, 1925 - .

[288] *The Freeman: organ of the Baptist denomination.* Leeds: J. Heaton [1855-6]; London: E. Marlborough, J. Heaton, Elliot Stock, 1855-1899. *The Baptist Times and Freeman:* London: E. Marlborough, J. Heaton, Elliot Stock, 1899-1925.

[289] Whitley, W.T. *The Baptists of London, 1612-1928: their fellowship, their expansion, with notes on their 850 churches.* London: Kingsgate Press, [1928?].

[290] Creasey, J. *Index to the John Evans List of dissenting congregations and ministers 1715-1729 in Dr Williams's library.* (Dr Williams's Library Occasional paper no. 11.) London: Dr Williams's Trust, 1964.

[291] 'A view of English nonconformity in 1773', *Transactions of the Congregational Historical Society,* vol. 5, 1911-12, pp. 205-222, 261-277.

[292] Wykes, D. Email to the author, 28.01.09.

[293] Langley, A.S. Baptist ministers in England about 1750 A.D. *Transactions of the Baptist Historical Society,* vol. 6, 1918-19, pp. 138-162.

[294] [Whitley, W.T.] An index to notable Baptists, whose careers began within the British Empire before 1850. *Transactions of the Baptist Historical Society*, 7, 1920-21, p. 182-239. Notable Baptists: Additions and corrections to the list in Volume VII. *Baptist Quarterly*, (New series) 1, 1922-23, p. 286-288.

[295] Shepherd, P. *The making of a northern Baptist college*. [Manchester]: Northern Baptist College, 2004. Short review in *Journal of European Baptist Studies*, 5(1), Sept. 2004, p. 64.

[296] Carter, A.C. *A popular sketch, historical and biographical, of the Midland Baptist College*. London: Kingsgate P., [1925]

[297] Nicholls, M. *Lights to the world: a history of Spurgeon's College 1856-1992*. Harpenden: in association with Nuprint, 1994.

[298] Randall, I.M. *A school of the prophets: 150 years of Spurgeon's College*. London: Spurgeon's College, 2005. Short review in *Baptist Quarterly*, 41(8), Oct. 2004, p. 512.

[299] Cooper, R.E. *From Stepney to St. Giles: the story of Regent's Park College, 1810-1960*. London: Carey Kingsgate P., 1960.

[300] Gould, G.P. *The Baptist College at Regent's Park: a centenary record*. London: Kingsgate P., 1910.

[301] Matthews, D.H. *From Abergavenny to Cardiff: history of the South Wales Baptist College (1806-2006)*. Abertawe [Swansea] : Gwasg Ilston, 2007.

[302] Jones, E.K. *The Baptists of Wales and ministerial education: also the nonconformist theological colleges of Wales*. Wrexham: Hughes, 1902.

[303] Moon, N. S. *Education for ministry: Bristol Baptist College 1679-1979*. Bristol: Bristol Baptist College, 1979.

[304] Swaine, S.A. *Faithful men: or, memorials of Bristol Baptist College, and some of its most distinguished alumni*. London: Alexander & Shepheard, 1884.

[305] Hayden, R. *Continuity and change: evangelical Calvinism among eighteenth-century Baptist ministers trained at Bristol Academy, 1690-1791*. Chipping Norton: Nigel Lynn for Roger Hayden and the Baptist Historical Society, 2006. Reviewed by Stephen Copson in *Baptist Quarterly* 42(2), April 2007, p. 177.

[306] Murray, D.B. *Scottish Baptist College: centenary history 1894-1994*. Glasgow: Scottish Baptist College, 1994.

4(b)(vii) Theses and dissertations

[307] *Index to theses [with abstracts] accepted for higher degrees by the universities of Great Britain and Ireland and the Council for National Academic Awards.* Quarterly. London: Aslib, 1970-1986, 1986 - . Previously *Index to theses accepted for higher degrees in the universities of Great Britain and Ireland,* 1953-1969.

[308] *Dissertation abstracts.* Monthly. Ann Arbor, Mich.: University Microfilms, 1952-1966. *Dissertation abstracts international. A, The humanities and social sciences.* Ann Arbor, Mich.: University Microfilms International, 1969 - . Also issued on CD-ROM.

[309] *Historical research for higher degrees in the United Kingdom.* Part I, Theses completed. Part II, Theses in progress. Published annually. London: University of London, Institute of Historical Research, 1986 - . Preceded by: *Historical research for university degrees in the United Kingdom.* Part I, Theses completed. Part II, Theses in progress. 1967-1984 and 1967-1985 respectively.

[310] Land, R.D. *Doctrinal controversies of English Particular Baptists (1644-1691) as illustrated by the career and writings of Thomas Collier.* Thesis (D.Phil.)--University of Oxford, 1980.

[311] MacDonald, M.D. *London Calvinistic Baptists, 1689-1727: tensions within a dissenting community under toleration.* Thesis (D.Phil.)--University of Oxford, 1983.

[312] Robison, O. *The Particular Baptists in England, 1760-1820.* Thesis (D.Phil.)--University of Oxford, 1963.

[313] Smith, K.E. *The community and the believer: a study of Calvinistic Baptist spirituality in some towns and villages of Hampshire and the borders of Wiltshire, c. 1730-1830.* Thesis (D.Phil.)--University of Oxford, 1987.

[314] Russell, H.O. *The missionary outreach of the West Indian church to West Africa in the nineteenth century with particular reference to the Baptists.* Thesis (D.Phil.)--University of Oxford, 1973.

[315] Bolt, C. *Some Evangelical missionaries' understanding of Negro character in Jamaica, 1834-1870; with particular reference to selected Baptist missionaries.* Thesis (Ph.D)--Oxford Centre for Mission Studies and University of Wales, 2006.

[316] Clifford, R.M. *The General Baptists, 1640-1660.* Thesis (M.Litt.)--University of Oxford, 1992.

[317] Cross, A. *The theology and practice of baptism amongst British Baptists 1900-1996.* Thesis (Ph.D)--Keele University, 1998.

[318] Dix, K. *Nineteenth century Strict Baptists.* Thesis (Ph.D)--Keele University, 1999.

[319] Nicholls, M. *The concept of ministry among Baptists 1850-1950.* Thesis (Ph.D)-- Keele University, 1999.

[320] Rinaldi, F.W. *The tribe of Dan: the New Connexion of General Baptists, 1770-1891: a study in the transition from revival movement to established denomination.* Thesis (Ph.D)--Glasgow University, 1996.

5(a) Primary sources: digital

[321] http://alexanderstreet.com/products/religion.htm

[322] http://solomon.tcpt.alexanderstreet.com/tcpt.about.html#1

[323] Ibid.

[324] http://eebo.chadwyck.com/marketing/about.htm

[325] http://www.intute.ac.uk/artsandhumanities/cgi-bin/search.pl?term1=Early+English+Books+Online&limit=0&subject=artsandhumanities&submit.x=11&submit.y=10

[326] http://www.gale.cengage.com/DigitalCollections/products/ecco/about.htm

[327] http://www.gale.cengage.com/DigitalCollections/products/ecco/find.htm

[328] http://www.intute.ac.uk/cgi-bin/search.pl?term1=Baptist+library+online&limit=0&subject=All&subject=artsandhumanities&submit.x=11&submit.y=11

[329] http://baptistlibraryonline.com/

[330] Carey, W. *An enquiry into the obligations of Christians to use means for the conversion of the heathens: in which the religious state of the different nations of the world, the success of former undertakings, and the practicability of further undertakings, are considered.* Leicester: Printed and sold by Ann Ireland [etc.], 1792. [later eds. 1818, 1892, 1934, 1961, 1991.] [electronic resource available]

[331] Cathcart, W., ed. *The Baptist Encyclopedia.* 2 v. Rev. ed. Philadelphia: Louis H. Everts, 1883.

[332] http://puritanism.online.fr/

[333] http://www.standardbearer.org/shop/Search.aspx?cat=ocdromand
http://www.standardbearer.org/shop/Search.aspx?cat=cdrom

[334] http://www.standardbearer.org/shop/Search.aspx?cat=ebk

5(b) Primary sources: printed facsimile or reprinted transcripts

[335] *Protestant Nonconformist texts*. 4 v. Aldershot: Ashgate, 2006 - 2007. Contents:
v. 1. 1550 to 1700; edited by R. Tudur Jones, with Arthur Long and Rosemary Moore
-- v. 2. The eighteenth century; edited by Alan P.F. Sell, with David J. Hall and Ian
Sellers -- v. 3. The nineteenth century; edited by David Bebbington; with Kenneth
Dix and Alan Ruston -- v. 4. The twentieth century; edited by David M. Thompson.
Vol. 1 reviewed by Stephen Copson in *Baptist Quarterly,* 42(8), Oct. 2008, p. 640.
Vol. 3 reviewed by John Briggs in *Baptist Quarterly*, 42(3), July 2007, p. 253. Vol. 4
reviewed by Keith Clements in *Baptist Quarterly,* 42(6), April 2008, p. 442.

[336] Ibid. Sell, A.P.F. Series note in each volume on pre-title page.

[337] Burrage, C. *The early English dissenters in the light of recent research (1550-
1641)*. 2 v. Cambridge: University Press, 1912.

[338] Lumpkin, W.L. *Baptist confessions of faith*. Chicago: Judson Press, [1959].

[339] Ibid.

[340] Smyth, J. *The works of John Smyth, Fellow of Christ's College, 1594-8*.
Tercentenary ed., with notes and biography by W.T. Whitley. Cambridge: Cambridge
University Press for the Baptist Historical Society, 1915.

[341] Helwys, T. *A short declaration of the mistery of iniquity..* [Amsterdam?: s.n.],
Anno 1612. STC (2nd ed.), 13056. ESTC, S4697. [Microfilm. Ann Arbor, Mich. :
University Microfilms International, 1985. 1 microfilm reel ; 35 mm. (Early English
books, 1475-1640 ; 1833:14).] Facsimile reprint published as *The mistery of iniquity*
London: Kingsgate Press for the Baptist Historical Society, 1935. A more modern
transcript, edited and introduced by Richard Groves, published by Mercer University
Press, c1998.

[342] Underhill, E.B., (ed.) *The records of a church of Christ meeting in Broadmead,
Bristol, 1640-1687*. London: J. Haddon for the Hanserd Knollys Society, 1847.

[343] Briggs, J.H.Y. and Sellers, I. (eds.) *Victorian nonconformity*. London: Edward
Arnold, 1973. (Documents of modern history)

[344] Thompson, D.M. (ed.) *Nonconformity in the nineteenth century*. London: Routledge & Kegan Paul, 1972.

[345] *Baptist Union documents, 1948-1977*; selected and introduced by Rev. Roger Hayden. London: Baptist Historical Society, 1980.

[346] Underhill, E.B. (ed.) *The bloudy tenent of persecution for cause of conscience discussed: and Mr Cotton's letter examined and answered by Roger Williams* (bound with the Second Annual Report of the Hanserd Knollys Society). London: J. Haddon for the Hanserd Knollys Society, 1848.

[347] Bunyan, J. *The pilgrim's progress: from this world to that which is to come*; edited [...] with an introduction by George Offor. London: J. Haddon, for The Hanserd Knollys Society, 1847.

[348] Underhill, E.B. (ed.) *Tracts on liberty of conscience and persecution, 1614-1661*. London: J. Haddon for the Hanserd Knollys Society, 1846.

[349] Underhill, E.B. (ed.) *A martyrology of the churches of Christ, commonly called Baptists, during the era of the Reformation*; translated from the Dutch of T.J. van Braght. London: J. Haddon and Son for the Hanserd Knollys Society, 1850-1853.

[350] Underhill, E.B. (ed.) *Confessions of faith and other public documents illustrative of the history of the Baptist Churches of England in the 17th century*. London: Haddon Brothers for the Hanserd Knollys Society, 1854.

[351] Whitley, W.T. (ed.) *Minutes of the General Assembly of the General Baptist churches in England: with kindred records*. London: Kingsgate Press for the Baptist Historical Society, [1909]-1910.

[352] Helwys, T. *The mistery of iniquity by Thomas Helwys of Gray's Inn and of Broxtowe Hall, Nottingham, 1612*. London: Kingsgate Press for the Baptist Historical Society, 1935. ("Reproduced ... from the copy presented by Helwys to King James, now in the Bodleian Library." With facsimile reproduction of original title page: A short declaration of the mistery of iniquity ... Anno 1612.)

[353] *General Baptist Assembly Occasional papers*, nos. 1 - 24, 1986-1995. Most transcriptions made by Leonard J. Maguire. Contents: v. 1. 1. History of Rushall General Baptist Church. 2. The retaining wall – Ditchling Meeting House. 3. The Baptist Meeting House Cuckfield Trust Deeds. 4. Ditchling Meeting House, notes by Emily Kensett. 5. The Charity of Philip Denning. 6. Swansea Meeting House. 7. Thomas Piety Trust – Ramsgate. 8. Bowles & Phillips Charities. 9. Chatham – Trust deeds. 10. Paul's Alley Church Book 1739-1768. 11. Canterbury Church Book 1711-1721. 12. Governing instruments & trust funds of the General Baptist Assembly. v. 2. 13. Church Book of Chatham 1801-1849. 14. Chatham Church – Register of Births, &c. 15. William Evershed's remarks. 16. Dover General Baptist Church. 17. Registers

of the Church at Canterbury. 18. Canterbury Church Book 1660-1695. 19. Diary of Peter Kensett 1819-1820. 20. William Evershed's sermon notes. 21. Diary of Peter Kensett 1819-1844. 22. A sermon preached for Mrs. Bull 1769. 23. Headcorn Church, Kent – Register of births, deaths &c 1731 to 1837. 24. Cranbrook Church, Kent – Register of births, deaths &c 1682 to 1837. [Further details in *Baptist Quarterly*, 40(3), July 2003, pp. [185]-187.]

354 McGlothlin, W.J. *Baptist confessions of faith*. Philadelphia: American Baptists Publication Society, 1911.

355 McBeth, L. *A sourcebook for Baptist heritage*. Nashville, Tenn.: Broadman Press, 1990.

356 Brackney, W.H. (ed.) *Baptist life and thought: a source book*. Rev. ed. Valley Forge, Pa.: Judson Press, 1998. ISBN: 0817012664.

357 Freeman, C.W. et al. *Baptist roots: a reader in the theology of a Christian people*. Valley Forge: Judson Press, c1999.

358 Helwys, T. *A short declaration of the mystery of iniquity*; edited by Richard Groves. Macon, Ga.: Mercer University Press, c1998.

359 Williams, R. *The bloudy tenant of persecution for cause of conscience;* ed. Richard Groves; historical intro. Edwin S. Gaustad. Macon, Ga.: Mercer University Press, [200-?] (Classics of Religious Liberty 2)

360 Dutton, A. *Selected spiritual writings of Anne Dutton: eighteenth-century, British-Baptist, woman theologian:* compiled and with an introduction by JoAnn Ford Watson. 5 v. Macon, Ga.: Mercer University Press, 2003- .

361 Early, J., Jr. *Readings in Baptist history*. Nashville: B&H Academic, 2008.

362 http://www.baptisttheology.org/ReadingsinBaptistHistory.cfm

363 Haykin, M.A.G. (ed.) *The British Particular Baptists, 1638-1910*. 3 v. Springfield, MO: Particular Baptist Press, c1998-2003.

364 Kinghorn, J. *The life and works of Joseph Kinghorn*; edited by Terry Wolever. 2 v. (of ultimate 4 v.) Springfield, MO: Particular Baptist Press, 1995- .

365 Booth, A. *The works of Abraham Booth;* edited by Michael A.G. Haykin with Alison E. Haykin. Springfield, Mo.: Particular Baptist Press, 2006-

5(c) Printed source documents

5(c)(i) Periodicals

[366] Taylor, R. *'English Baptist periodicals, 1790-1865: a bibliography and survey'.* Thesis (M.Phil.)--University of London, 1974.

[367] Taylor, R. 'English Baptist periodicals, 1790-1865'. *Baptist Quarterly,* 27(2), April 1977, p. 50-82.

[368] Taylor, R. *Baptist Quarterly,* 27(2), ibid. p. 53.

[369] Manley, K. *'Redeeming love proclaim'.* Op. cit., p. 149-150.

[370] Breed, G.R. *Particular Baptists in Victorian England and their Strict Communion organizations.* Didcot: Baptist Historical Society, 2003. pp. 318-319. Reviewed by Alan P.F. Sell in *Baptist Quarterly* 40(8), Oct. 2004, p. 500-501.

[371] *The General Baptist Magazine,* vols.1-3, London, 1798-1800. *The General Baptist Repository,* vols. 1-10, n.s.1-12, n.s.1-5, 1-14, London, 1802-1853. *The General Baptist Magazine (Repository) and missionary observer,* vols. 1-6, n.s.1-93, London, 1854-91. Followed by the *Baptist Union Magazine,* vols. 1-2, 1892-3.

[372] *Minutes of an Association of General Baptists [of the New Connexion] held at... 1785-1868,* succeeded by *The General Baptist Year Book (Year Book & Minutes), 1869-1891)* [Vol.1 *Minutes of the General Baptist Association, held at Boston, Lincolnshire; April 27th and 28th 1785.* London: Printed by J. Brown.] [Various titles, including *Minutes of an Association of General Baptist ministers and representatives of churches, holden at ... ",* and imprints.].

[373] Taylor, R. op. cit. *Baptist Quarterly,* 27(2), p. 56-7.

[374] *Scottish Baptist Magazine.* Glasgow: Baptist Union of Scotland, 1875-1984.

[375] *The Irish Baptist Magazine.* Belfast: William W. Cleland. Vols. 1- 30, no. 3. Jan. 1877-March, 1906.

[376] *(The) Missionary Herald.* London: G. Wightman; Baptist Missionary Society, 1819-2000. Continued as *World Mission,* 2001- .

[377] *The Baptist Messenger: an(d) evangelical treasury and chronicle of the churches.* London: B.L. Green, James Paul, April 1854-1899.

[378] Taylor, R. op cit. *Baptist Quarterly,* 27(2), p. 72.

[379] *The Gospel Herald.* Vols. 1-54, London, 1833-1886. 1887-1918 as *The Earthen Vessel and Gospel Herald.* Vols. 75-138, 1919-1970. as *The Gospel Herald and Earthen Vessel.*

[380] *The Earthen Vessel: (and Christian Record).* Vols.1-67. London, 1845-1916. 1887-1918 as *The Earthen Vessel and Gospel Herald.; continued as The Gospel Herald and Earthen Vessel.*

[381] *The Gospel Standard, [or Feeble Christian's support].* v. 1- . Manchester: J. Gadsby; London: E. Fowler, 1835- . [Various printers, including in 1980s Chandlers, Bexhill-on-Sea.]

[382] Cox, S. *Salvator mundi: or, is Christ the Saviour of all men?* London: Henry S. King, 1877.

[383] Former Historical Commission, Southern Baptist Convention, Microfilm pub. No. 573. Not found on current site http://www.sbhla.org/microfilm.htm.

[384] *The Baptist: a family newspaper for the Baptist denomination.* London: Elliot Stock, 1873-1883.

[385] Manley, K. *'Redeeming love proclaim' :* op. cit., p. 294.

5(c)(ii) Association reports and circular letters

[386] *A brief historical account of the churches in the Association. The Circular letter of the West-Riding of Yorkshire Association of Baptist churches assembled in Rochdale, on Tuesday, Wednesday and Thursday May 17th, 18th and 19th, 1842; maintaining generally the important doctrines ... to the members of those several churches also, the report of the annual meeting of the Yorkshire and Lancashire Baptist Itinerant Society, for the year ending May 31st, 1842.* Leeds: printed by John Heaton, 1842.

[387] The Circular letter from the ministers and messengers, assembled at Oulney in Bucks, June 15 and 16, 1768 ... . p. 1.

[388] *Qualifications for church fellowship: the circular letter from the ministers and messengers of the several Baptist Churches of the Northamptonshire Association, assembled at Nottingham, June 3, 4, 5, 1800. p. 1.*

5(c)(iii) Tracts, sermons

[389] Breed, G.R. *Particular Baptists in Victorian England* .... Op. cit., pp. 214-282.

[390] Angus Library 4.h.28-36.

[391] Angus Library 5.g.13

[392] Angus Library Z.a.11

[393] Angus Library 36.a.12A and 36.a.12B. Spine titles: *Spurgeon et al. Baptismal regeneration controversy.*

[394] Angus Library 11.e.28 – 11.e.34.

[395] *New Park Street Pulpit: containing sermons preached and revised by C.H.Spurgeon...1855 (-1860).* London, 1856-1861.

[396] *Metropolitan Tabernacle Pulpit: sermons preached by C. H. Spurgeon.* London: Passmore & Alabaster, 1864-1901.

[397] Hebden, S. *Baptismal regeneration disproved; the scripture account of the nature of regeneration explained; and the absolute necessity of such a change argued from the native corruption of man since the fall; in a discourse on John III. 5,6.* London: printed for R. Hett; and J. Oswald, 1741. ESTC T66261. (Electronic reproduction of original from the British Library. Farmington Hills, Mich: Thomson Gale, 2003. Available via the World Wide Web. Access limited by licensing agreements.)

5(d) Manuscripts

5(d)(i) Guides

[398] Steel, D.J. *Sources for nonconformist genealogy and family history.* London: Society of Genealogists, 1973. (National index of parish registers).

[399] Shorney, D. *Protestant nonconformity and Roman Catholicism: a guide to sources in the Public Record Office.* London: PRO Publications, 1996. (Public Record Office readers' guide no. 13)

[400] Gandy, M. *Tracing nonconformist ancestors.* Richmond: Public Record Office, 2001.

[401] Gandy, M. *Basic facts about English nonconformity for family historians.* Birmingham: Federation of Family History Societies, 1998.

[402] McLaughlin, E. *Nonconformist ancestors*. Haddenham: Varneys Press, 1995.

[403] Palgrave-Moore, P. *Understanding the history and records of nonconformity*. 2nd ed. [Norwich]: Elvery Dowers, 1988.

[404] Park, K. *Non-conformist records*. Mountain Ash: Knowledge Base Publications, 1995. (Family history fact finder series, no. 15)

[405] Ruston, A.R. *Nonconformity in Hertfordshire: a guide to sources for family and local historians*. Barnet: Hertfordshire Family History Society, 2005. (Hertfordshire Family History Society Special Publication, no. 6)

[406] *Tracing your family history in Hertfordshire*. Hatfield: Hertfordshire Pubns. for Hertfordshire Archives and Local Studies (HALS), 2003.

[407] Jones, G. *The descent of Dissent: a guide to the Nonconformist records at the Leicestershire Record Office*. Leicester: Leicestershire Museums, Arts and Record Service, 1989. (Leicestershire Museums Publication, no. 102)

[408] *Nonconformist records: a brief introduction*. Kingston upon Thames: Surrey Record Office, c1988.

[409] Ward, G. *Sources for Researching Nonconformists in Northamptonshire*. [Northampton]: Northamptonshire Family History Society, 2004.

[410] http://website.lineone.net/~gsward/index.html

5(d)(ii) Local church records

[411] http://www.baptist.org.uk/baptist_life/baptist_family/national/corporation.html

[412] Underhill, E.B. (ed.) *Records of the churches of Christ, gathered at Fenstanton, Warboys, and Hexham, 1644-1720*. London: Hanserd Knollys Society, 1854.

[413] Hayden, R. (ed.) *The records of a church of Christ in Bristol, 1640-1687*. Gateshead: printed for the Bristol Record Society, 1974.

[414] *The General Baptist Church of Berkhamsted, Chesham and Tring 1712-1781*, transcribed by L.G. Champion. [London]: Baptist Historical Society, 1985. (English Baptist Records, 1)

[415] *Church book: St Andrew's Street Baptist Church, Cambridge 1720-1832; [*Robert Robinson ; transcribed by L.G. Champion]. [London]: Baptist Historical Society, 1991. (English Baptist Records, 2)

416
http://www.nationalarchives.gov.uk/searchthearchives/default.htm?source=ddmenu_s
earch0 Reproduced with the permission of The National Archives.

417 http://www.nationalarchives.gov.uk/a2a/about.aspx Reproduced with the
permission of The National Archives.

418 http://www.nationalarchives.gov.uk/nra/aboutapps/nra/about.htm Reproduced with
the permission of The National Archives.

419 http://www.nationalarchives.gov.uk/catalogue/about.asp#search Reproduced with
the permission of The National Archives.

5(d)(iii) Association and other organizational records

420 Briggs, J.H.Y. *The English Baptists of the nineteenth century*. Op. cit., p. 199.

421 White, B.R.(ed.) *Association records of the Particular Baptists of England, Wales
and Ireland to 1660*. 3 parts + Index. London: Baptist Historical Society, 1971-4.

422 Nuttall, G.F. 'Assembly and Association in Dissent, 1689-1831', in *Councils and
assemblies: papers read at the eighth summer meeting and the ninth winter meeting
of the Ecclesiastical History Society*; edited by G.J. Cuming and Derek Baker.
Cambridge: University Press, 1971. (*Studies in church history*, 7) p. 289-309.

423 Briggs, J.H.Y. *The English Baptists of the nineteenth century*. Op. cit., pp. 199-
247.

424 Midland Association circular letters, 1715-1772, originally in the possession of
Bewdley Baptist Church. Ms. Angus Library ref. F.P.C. E7.

425 Particular Baptist Fund: 1717-1980: correspondence, minutes, accounts,
distributions, rent books, fund books, legacies and donations, reports. NRA ref. no.
33494 Particular. Angus Library D/PBF.

426 Particular Baptist Fund: Fund Book I, 1717-1729. ms. (Spelling modernised)
Angus Library D/PBF 1.

427 *Bristol Baptist Fund, 1717-1958*. [Bristol: Bristol Baptist Fund, 1958?]

428 Baptist Union of Great Britain (and Ireland). Council and main committee minutes:
1812-1975 (as at 2008) + some separate index volumes. Ms. Angus Library.

429 An account of the proceedings of the Society of Baptist Ministers in London from
17 August 1714 to 16 August 1736. Ms. Angus Library.

[430] General Baptist Building Fund. Minutes, 1866-1890. Ms. Angus Library.

[431] The Association Book belonging to the New Connexion of General Baptists, 1797-1826. Minutes of the Annual Association of the New Connexion of General Baptists, 1833-58, 1959-71, 1872-86, 1887-1938. General Baptists of the New Connexion, Conference minutes, 1770-1798. General Baptists New Connexion, Lincolnshire Conference: minute book of the quarterly meetings, 1791-1803. Lancs. and Yorks. General Baptist conference, 1873-1891. Midland Conference minute book, 1859-1891. General Baptists Yorkshire District: minute book of quarterly conference, 1841-1873. Ms. Angus Library.

[432] Baptist Board: Minute books, 1723-1817, 1818-35, 1835-72, 1872-91, 1932-43, 1944-1951, 1952-1965, 1964-72; Committee minutes 1964-72. 1st vol. entitled "The Minutes of a Society of Ministers of the Baptist Particular persuasion Meeting at the Gloucestershire Coffee House on Mondays at three a'clock", Jan.20th, 1723 – Sep.16, 1817; 2nd vol: "Extracts from the Minutes of a Society of Particular Baptist ministers in London and its environs": summary 1723, minutes 1818-1835. 3rd vol.: "The Minutes of the Board of Particular Baptist ministers who first met at the Gloucestershire Coffee House. Subsequently at the Jamaica Coffee House. But who from July 1th 1823 have met at Fen Court, London." [This gives the contents of the two preceding volumes and Minutes from the Annual meeting March 17th, 1835 – April 23rd, 1872.] Ms. Angus Library. First 2 vols. transcribed and annotated [presumably by W.T. Whitley] in the *Transactions of the Baptist Historical Society*, vols. V, 1916-17, p. 96-114 (1723-1727), p. 197-240 (1728-1750), VI, 1918-19, p.72-127 (1750-1820), and VII, 1920-21, p. 49-70 (1820-1835).

[433] London: Baptist Monthly Meeting. The minute book of the Baptist Monthly Meeting ... 1748-1829. Ms. Angus Library.

[434] London Baptist Property Board. Directors' minutes, 8.5.1906-11.9.1934; 3 v. Ms. Register of leases, 1857-1921 and other documents. Angus Library. Later records retained by the Board.

[435] London Association of Strict Baptist Ministers and Churches: Minute book, 1846-53. Ms. Angus Library.

[436] London Baptist Preachers' Association: Minutes, 1905-14, 1933-2005, plus some membership material. Ms. Angus Library.

[437] Baptist Irish Society. Minutes (final copy): 1832-44, 1844-51, 1858-65, 1865-70; Rough draft Committee minutes, 1836-46. Ms. Angus Library.

[438] Minutes of the proceedings of the Baptist Society in London for the encouragement and support of Itinerant Preaching. 1797-1812. Ms. BMS Archive, Angus Library.

[439] *Baptists together in Christ, 1905-2005,* op. cit., p. 331.

5(d)(iv) Baptist colleges' records

[440] General Baptist Education society. Minutes Feb. 1st 1825- June 6th, 1861. (Includes "Plan of the GB Education Society")

[441] Nottingham Baptist College, Chilwell: Minutes 1861-91, 1891-1912. 2 v. Ms. Angus Library.

[442] Shepherd, P. *The making of a northern Baptist college,* op. cit. p. 283.

[443] Newman, William (1773-1835) Diaries, 1808-14, 1820-25, 1825-33,1833-34. 4 v. Ms. Angus Library, Z.k.1-4. NRA catalogue ref. 20044.

5(d)(v) Baptist Missionary Society

[444] Stanley, B. *The history of the Baptist Missionary Society, 1792-1992.* Edinburgh: T&T Clark, 1992.

[445] George Grenfell: Survey books of Lunda Expeditions, 1885-1905. BMS Archive Boxes A/24-26.

[446] Roxburgh, W. *Hortus Bengalensis.* Serampore: The Mission Press, 1814. Copy in BMS Archive annotated by William Carey. IN/13

[447] e.g. the correspondence of Alfred G. Jones, BMS Archive CH/5-8 and Timothy Richard, CH/2-4, specifically letters dating from 1900.

[448] e.g. the correspondence of William Knibb, BMS Archive WI/3, but see also Angus Library outside the BMS Archive the Fenn Collection of papers at D/FEN.

[449] BMS Archive, W. Holman Bentley's letters to BMS Secretary Baynes dated 1888-1889 referring to Casement's employment as a lay helper at the Wathen Mission Station for 3-4 months, A/31/3 (xvi), A/31/4 (ii and iii). Letters from Casement to Bentley A/34/5 (i-iii).

[450] BMS Archive, correspondence of George Grenfell. Letters dated 15 July, 1901 enclosing letter from Casement dated 5 June 1901, A/20/2 (xvii) and (xviii); Grenfell's 1903 correspondence with Roger Casement, A/21/12 (i-iii).

[451] Briggs, J. Editorial review, *Baptist Quarterly,* 40(3), July 2003, p. 132.

[452] Farrer, K.T.H. *William Carey: missionary and botanist.* Kew, Victoria: Carey Baptist Grammar School, 2005. Reviewed by John Briggs in *Baptist Quarterly* 42 (2 Pt.2), April 2007, p. 183-4.

[453] Carey, W. *The journal and selected letters of William Carey*; collected and edited by Terry G. Carter. Macon, Ga.: Smyth & Helwys, c2000. Reviewed by John Briggs in *Baptist quarterly* 41 (1), Jan. 2005, p. 59-60.

[454] Southern Baptist Historical Library and Archives. *Guide to microfilm of Baptist Missionary Society Archives, London, England, 1792-1914.* Microfilm publication no. 5350. Nashville, Te., [198-?] Copy at http://www.sbhla.org/downloads/mf_5350.pdf

[455] Minutes of Transactions at the Meetings of the Committee of the General Baptist missionary Society instituted at Boston 1816. 1816-1861. Ms.

[456] Original letters, 1736-1779. Sutcliff Papers. Bound vol. Mss.

[457] The Down Grade controversy and the Rev. C.H. Spurgeon, 1887-89. Bound volume containing printed articles and ms. letters mounted as in a scrapbook.

[458] Whelan, T. 'A chronological calendar of Baptist autographs at the John Rylands University Library of Manchester, 1741-1907,' *Baptist Quarterly,* 42(8), Oct. 2008, p. 577-612.

[459] North Yorkshire County Record Office. Marshman family papers 1747-1872 [MIC 1467-8] General Sir Henry Havelock: letters to his wife Hannah 1854-55. [MIC 1770] within the HAVELOCK-ALLAN OF BLACKWELL ARCHIVES, ref. ZDG. See

http://www.nationalarchives.gov.uk/a2a/records.aspx?cat=191-zdg&cid=0&kw=Marshman#0 or
http://archives.northyorks.gov.uk/DServe/dserve.exe?dsqIni=Dserve.ini&dsqApp=Archive&dsqCmd=Show.tcl&dsqDb=Catalog&dsqPos=1&dsqSearch=((text)='Marshman')

[460] Missionaries at Serampore. IOR/H/690 1807 British Library, Asia, Pacific and Africa Collections

5(d)(vi) Miscellaneous manuscripts

[461] Isaac Mann: collection of letters; &c. 1711-1831, National Library of Wales, MS 1207E see http://cat.llgc.org.uk/cgi-bin/gw/chameleon . "Calendar of letters, 1742-1831, collected by Isaac Mann", [compiled by F.G. Hastings, with annotations by

W.T. Whitley]. *Baptist Quarterly,* 6, 1932-3, pp. 39-43, 83-85, 173-186, 218-226, 277-283, 318-322, 373-379, and 7, 1933-4, pp. 39-46, 89-91, 138-9, 175-185, 235-238. The collection is also collated with T.Whelan's Calendar of Baptist autographs in Manchester, noted above. A microfilm copy of this collection is available for consultation in the Angus Library, Regent's Park College, Oxford.

[462] Isaac Mann Autograph Collection. James Marshall and Marie-Louise Osborn Collection, Beinecke Rare Book and Manuscript Library, Yale University. OSB MSS 46. See http://webtext.library.yale.edu/xml2html/beinecke.manni.con.html#a8. "Isaac Mann's Collection of letters": *Baptist Quarterly*, 26, 1975-6, p. 134-139. A microfilm copy of this collection is available for consultation in the Angus Library, Regent's Park College, Oxford.

[463] Whelan, T. *Baptist autographs at the John Rylands University Library of Manchester, 1741-1845.* (Forthcoming. Macon, Ga.: Mercer University Press, 2009.)

[464] Birmingham University Information Services, Special Collections Department. Pashkov Papers [1812-1909] - ref. VP http://www.nationalarchives.gov.uk/a2a/records.aspx?cat=150-vp&cid=0#0 A microfiche copy of the collection is now held by the International Baptist Theological Seminary in Prague (see http://www.ibts.eu/news item noted 10.11.2008) and also at the Southern Baptist Historical Library and Archives in the USA, which has listed the collection at http://www.sbhla.org/downloads/115m.pdf

[465] Lambeth Palace Library. Several collections containing correspondence between Melbourn Evans Aubrey, General Secretary of the Baptist Union of Great Britain and Ireland and Archbishops William Temple and George Bell, e.g. W.Temple 58, ff. 1-37, WAR 1939-45, 2 Mar-16 Oct 1944: Papers relating to publication of statements by the Peace Aims Group, including correspondence from: ... Melbourn Evans Aubrey; Bell 214, ff. 147, 152-3: Correspondence with Melbourn Evans Aubrey, General Secretary, and (1950) President of the Baptist Union of Great Britain and Ireland; MS 3061 ff. 23-35: Memorandum by the Revd Melbourn Evans Aubrey, General Secretary of the Baptist Union, on the effects of disestablishment in British possessions overseas and in the United States (C.C.S. 77). See http://80.169.35.2:8080/Archives/index.htm .

[466] British Library, Manuscript Collections. Add. 25,386-25,389. Letters to John Rippon, D.D., Baptist minister; 1769-1839. 4 v. Paper. Folio.

[467] Ryland, John (1753-1825) Baptist Minister, 1766-1825: correspondence, notebooks, MSS. Northamptonshire Record Office, 1978/168. NRA catalogue reference 8563 Northampton Baptist.

[468] Norfolk Record Office. MC 64 includes "Two letters from the Rev. Andrew Leslie, Baptist Missionary at Serampore, India, to Thomas Theobald, St Saviour's, Norwich". MC 64/2, 1824; Letter "from George Kinghorn Prince, Bideford, Devon, to M. H.

Wilkin, re George Kinghorn (d.1823) and giving names of local Baptists to whom
Wilkin's prospectus (presumably of his biography of Joseph Kinghorn) might be sent"
MC 64/3, 1854; and "Notes and papers of C.B. Jewson, mostly relating to Baptist
history and radical and philosophical movements in Norfolk in the late 18th and early
19th centuries. [no ref. or date]" MC 64/4,. See
http://www.nationalarchives.gov.uk/a2a/records.aspx?cat=153-mc64&cid=-1 and
http://nrocat.norfolk.gov.uk/Dserve/public/nrosearches.htm .

[469] Steele family papers. Angus Library D/STE 1 – D/STE 14. NRA 35753.

[470] Angus Library D/STE 5/5.

[471] William Carey Collection [family correspondence] Angus Library WCC/1. NRA
33492 Also miscellaneous correspondence NRA 20044 .

[472] Angus family archive. Angus Library (no reference no. yet allocated).

[473] Correspondence 1790-1832 of Joseph Kinghorn (1766-1832). Angus Library
D/KIN [formerly 4/3/1-3]. NRA 33498.

[474] Papers of James Henry Rushbrooke (1870-1947). Angus Library D/RUS. NRA
33952

[475] Reeves Collection. Angus Library. (no collection reference yet allocated;
documents referenced with R)

[476] Gould manuscript Angus Library D/GOU 1

[477] Stinton, B. *A repository of divers historical matters* Angus Library D/STI 1. The
term has also sometimes been used to refer to *A Journal of the Affairs of ye
Antipaedobaptists beginning with ye Reign of King George whose Accession to the
Throne was on the first of August 1714.* Angus Library ref. 3.h.30.

[478] Abingdon manuscript Angus Library D/AA 1

[479] Kreitzer, L.J. '1653 or 1656: when did Oxford Baptists join the Abingdon
Association', in Thompson, P.E. and Cross, A.R. (eds.): *Recycling the past or
researching history?: studies in Baptist historiography and myths.* Milton Keynes:
Paternoster, 2005, p. 207-219.

Appendix

[480] Nuttall, G.F. 'Assembly and Association in Dissent, 1689-1831', op cit., pp. 289-
309.

[481] Briggs, J.H.Y. *The English Baptists of the nineteenth century.* Op. cit., Chapter 7,
'Associations, alliances and the wider church, pp. 199-247.

ALPHABETICAL LIST OF PRINTED SOURCES EXCLUDING PERIODICAL TITLES AND UNPUBLISHED THESES

Note: Some references are cited in a more complete form in the list of references than here. The form of description is not entirely according to Library of Congress cataloguing principles, in particular in the case of headings under personal editors and the capitalisation of periodical titles. The capitalisation of only the first word of a title and proper nouns accords with standard library cataloguing principles.

Andronoviene, L. *Involuntarily free or voluntarily bound: singleness in the Baptistic communities of post-communist Europe.* Praha: International Baptist Theological Seminary of the European Baptist Federation, 2003.

"As witness this day": Princes Risborough Baptist Church, 1707-2007; a celebration. [Princes Risborough: Princes Risborough Baptist Church, 2007.]

Atanda, J.A. (ed.) *Baptist churches in Nigeria, 1850-1950: accounts of their foundation and growth.* Ibadan: University Press, 1988.

Balders, G. (ed.) *Ein Herr, ein Glaube, eine Taufe: 150 Jahre Baptistengemeinden in Deutschland, 1834-1984.* 2nd ed. Wuppertal: Oncken, 1985.

Baptist World Congress: London, July 11-19, 1905; authorized record of proceedings with introduction by J.H. Shakespeare. London: Baptist Union Publication Department, 1905.

Baptists in Yorkshire, Lancashire, Cheshire & Cumberland. London: Kingsgate Press, 1913.

Bassett, T.M. The Baptists of Wales and the Baptist Missionary Society. Swansea: Ilston Press, 1991.

Bassett, T.M. *The Welsh Baptists.* Swansea: Ilston House, 1977.

Bebbington, D.W. *Evangelicalism in modern Britain : a history from the 1730s to the 1980s.* London: Routledge, 1993.

Bebbington, D.W. (ed.) *The Baptists in Scotland: a history.* Glasgow: Baptist Union of Scotland, 1988.

Bebbington, D.W. (ed.) *The Gospel in the world: international Baptist studies.* Carlisle: Paternoster, 2002.

Bell, M.R. *Apocalypse how?: Baptist movements during the English Revolution.* Macon, Ga.: Mercer U. P., c2000.

Binfield, C. *Pastors and people: the biography of a Baptist church, Queen's Road Coventry.* Coventry: Queen's Road Baptist Church, 1984.

Larsen T. (ed.) *Biographical dictionary of evangelicals.* Leicester: Inter-Varsity Press, 2003.

Boase, F. *Modern English biography, containing many thousand concise memoirs of persons who have died between the years of 1851-1900: with an index of the most interesting matter.* 6 v. [London]: Cass, 1965. (Reprint of 1st ed. published Netherton & Worth, 1892-1921)

Bonsall, H.E. with Robertson, E.H. *The dream of an ideal city: Westbourne Park, 1877-1977.* London: Westbourne Park Baptist Church; York: Sessions, 1978.

Booth, A. *The works of Abraham Booth;* edited by Michael A.G. Haykin with Alison E. Haykin. Springfield, Mo.: Particular Baptist Press, 2006-

Bowers, F. *A bold experiment: the story of Bloomsbury Chapel and Bloomsbury Central Baptist Church, 1848-1999.* London: Bloomsbury Central Baptist Church, 1999.

Brackney, W.H. (ed.) *Baptist life and thought: a source book.* Rev. ed. Valley Forge, Pa.: Judson Press, 1998.

Brackney, W.H. *The Baptists.* New York: Greenwood, 1988.

Brackney, W.H. *Baptists in North America: an historical perspective.* Oxford: Blackwell, 2006.

Brackney, W.H. *Christian voluntarism in Britain and North America: a bibliography and critical assessment.* Westport, Conn.: Greenwood Press, 1995.

Brackney, W.H. *A genetic history of Baptist thought: with special reference to Baptists in Britain and North America*. Macon, GA: Mercer University Press, 2004.

Brackney, W.H. *Historical dictionary of the Baptists*. Lanham, Md. : Scarecrow Press, 1999.

Brackney, W.H., Fiddes, P.S. and Briggs, J.H.Y. (eds.) *Pilgrim pathways: essays in Baptist history in honour of B.R. White*. Macon, Ga.: Mercer University Press, c1999.

Breed, G.R. *My ancestors were Baptists: how can I find out more about them?* Rev. ed. London: Society of Genealogists, 2007.

Breed, G.R. *Particular Baptists in Victorian England and their Strict Communion organizations*. Didcot: Baptist Historical Society, 2003.

Brewer, J. *An outline history of the General Baptists of Loughborough, 1760 to 1975*. Loughborough: the author, 1979.

Briggs, J.H.Y. and Sellers, I. (eds.) *Victorian nonconformity*. London: Edward Arnold, 1973.

Briggs, J.H.Y. *The English Baptists of the nineteenth century*. Didcot: Baptist Historical Society, c1994.

Bristol Baptist Fund, 1717-1958. [Bristol: Bristol Baptist Fund, 1958?]

Brown, K.D. *A social history of the nonconformist ministry in England and Wales, 1800-1930*. Oxford: Clarendon Press, 1988.

Brown, R. *The English Baptists of the eighteenth century*. London: Baptist Historical Society, c1986.

Browne, J. *History of Congregationalism and memorials of the churches in Norfolk and Suffolk*. London: Jarrold and Sons, 1877.

Buffard, F. *Kent and Sussex Baptist Associations*. Faversham: E. Vinson, [1964].

Bunyan, J. *The pilgrim's progress: from this world to that which is to come*; edited [...] with an introduction by George Offor. London: J. Haddon, for The Hanserd Knollys Society, 1847.

Burrage, C. *The early English dissenters in the light of recent research (1550-1641).* 2 v. Cambridge: University Press, 1912.

Calamy, E. (rev. Palmer, S.) *The Nonconformist's memorial: being an account of the ministers, who were ejected or silenced after the Restoration, particularly by the Act of Uniformity, ... Aug. 24, 1662.* 2nd ed. London: 1775-8.

Cannon, J., ed. A *dictionary of British History.* Oxford University Press, 2004.

Cannon, J., ed. *The Oxford companion to British history.* Rev. ed. Oxford University Press, 2002.

Carey, W. *An enquiry into the obligations of Christians to use means for the conversion of the heathens: in which the religious state of the different nations of the world, the success of former undertakings, and the practicability of further undertakings, are considered.* Leicester: Printed and sold by Ann Ireland ..., 1792. [later eds. 1818,1892,1934,1961,1991.]

Carey, W. *The journal and selected letters of William Carey*; collected and edited by Terry G. Carter. Macon, Ga.: Smyth & Helwys, c2000.

Carlile, J.C. *The story of the English Baptists.* London: James Clarke, 1905.

Carter, A.C. *A popular sketch, historical and biographical, of the Midland Baptist College.* London: Kingsgate P., [1925]

Cathcart, W., ed. *The Baptist Encyclopedia.* 2 v. Rev. ed. Philadelphia: Louis H. Everts, 1883.

Chadwick, R.E. *Sacred ground, high tradition: Salendine Nook Baptist Church 1743-1993.* [s.l.: s.n., 1993]

Chadwick, R.E. (ed.) *A Protestant Catholic church of Christ: essays on the history and life of New Road Baptist Church, Oxford.* Oxford: New Road Baptist Church, 2003.

Chadwick, R.E. and Joynes, D.W. *'Persistent efforts and untiring labours': Beulah Baptist Church, Hollinwood, Oldham 1891-1991.* [Hollinwood: Printed by the Commercial Centre, 1991?]

Chambers Scottish biographical dictionary. Edinburgh: Chambers, 1992.

Chambers, R.F. et al. *The Strict Baptist chapels of England*. 5 v. London: Strict Baptist Historical Society, 1952-1968.

Champion, L.G. (ed.) *Church book: St Andrew's Street Baptist Church, Cambridge 1720-1832*. [London]: Baptist Historical Society, 1991.

Champion, L.G. (ed.) *The General Baptist Church of Berkhamsted, Chesham and Tring 1712-1781*. [London]: Baptist Historical Society, 1985.

Clark, W.P. *Eythorne: our Baptist heritage*. [Sandwich: W. Philip Clark, 1981]

Coleman, H.J. *Russian Baptists and spiritual revolution, 1905-1929*. Bloomington, Ind.: Indiana University Press, 2005.

Collis, M.J. *Shropshire Baptist history: an account of the Baptist churches of Shropshire and surrounding areas*. Shropshire Group of Baptist Churches, 2008.

Cooper, R.E. *From Stepney to St. Giles: the story of Regent's Park College, 1810-1960*. London: Carey Kingsgate P., 1960.

Copeland, D.A. *Benjamin Keach and the development of Baptist traditions in seventeenth-century England*. Lewiston, N.Y.; Lampeter: Edwin Mellen Press, c2001.

Copson, S.L. *Association life of the Particular Baptists of Northern England 1699-1732*. [London]: Baptist Historical Society, 1991.

Corrado, S. and Pilli, T. (eds.) *Eastern European Baptist history: new perspectives*. Praha: International Baptist Theological Seminary of the European Baptist Federation, 2007.

Couling, S. *The dead in Christ, or, The Baptists in Bunhill Fields*. London: Baptist Tract Society, [1871?]

Cox, S. *Salvator mundi: or, is Christ the Saviour of all men?* London: Henry S. King, 1877.

Cramer, S.A. *Loughborough Baptists and the town*. Loughborough Baptist Church, 2000.

Cramp, J.M. *Baptist history from the foundation of the Christian church to the close of the eighteenth century*. London: Elliot Stock, 1868.

Creasey, J. *Index to the John Evans List of dissenting congregations and ministers 1715-1729 in Dr. Williams's library.* (Dr. Williams's Library Occasional paper no. 11.) London: Dr. Williams's Trust, 1964.

Crone, J.S. *A concise dictionary of Irish biography.* Rev. ed. Dublin: Talbot Press, 1937.

Crosby, T. *The history of the English Baptists, from the Reformation to the beginning of the reign of King George I.* 4 v. London: printed for, and sold by, the editor, 1738-1740.

Deacon, S. *Memoirs of the late Mr. Samuel Deacon: who was nearly forty years pastor and fifty years a member of the General Baptist Church, Barton, Leicestershire; with extracts from his various writings, letters, &c.* Loughborough: printed and sold at the General Baptist Printing-Office, [1827?]

Devine, J and Egger-Sider, F. *Going beyond Google: the invisible web in learning and teaching.* London: Facet Publishing, 2009.

Dictionary of Scottish biography. Irvine: Carrick Media, c1999- .

Dictionary of Welsh biography down to 1940. London: Honourable Society of Cymmrodorion, 1959.

Dictionary of Welsh biography, 1941-1970: together with a supplement to The dictionary of Welsh biography down to 1940. London: Honourable Society of Cymmrodorion, 2001.

Dix, Kenneth. *Strict and Particular: English Strict and Particular Baptists in the nineteenth century.* Didcot: Baptist Historical Society for the Strict Baptist Historical Society, c2001.

Doel, W. *Twenty golden candlesticks: or a history of Baptist nonconformity in western Wiltshire.* Trowbridge: Lansdown and Rose; London: Simpkin, Marshall, ..., 1890. Facsimile reprint 2005.

Douglas, D. *History of the Baptist churches in the North of England: from 1648 to 1845.* London: Houlston and Stoneman, 1846.

Dr. Williams's Library. *Catalogue of the Library in Red Cross Street, Cripplegate, founded pursuant to the will of Daniel Williams, who died in the year 1716.* 2 v. London: Richard & John E. Taylor, 1841. Vol. 3 Woodfall & Kinder, 1854. Catalogues of accessions, 1900-1950, 1951-1960, 1961-1970, 1971-1980. London: Dr. Williams's Trust, 1955, 1961, 1972, 1983.

Dr. Williams's Library. *Nonconformist congregations in Great Britain: a list of histories and other material in Dr. Williams's Library.* London: Dr. Williams's Trust, 1973.

Durso, P.R. and K.E. *The story of Baptists in the United States.* Brentwood, Tenn.: Baptist History and Heritage Society, 2006.

Dutton, A. *Selected spiritual writings of Anne Dutton: eighteenth-century, British-Baptist, woman theologian:* compiled and with an introduction by JoAnn Ford Watson. 5 v. Macon, Ga.: Mercer University Press, 2003- .

Early nonconformity, 1566-1800: a catalogue of books in Dr. Williams's Library, London. Author catalogue. Subject catalogue. Chronological catalogue. 12 v. Boston: G. K. Hall, 1968.

Early, J., Jr. *Readings in Baptist history.* **Nashville: B&H Academic, 2008.**

Elwyn, T.H.S. *The Northamptonshire Baptist Association.* London: Carey Kingsgate Press, 1964.

Evans, B. *The early English Baptists.* London: J. Heaton & Son, 1862.

Evans, G.E. *Come wind, come weather: chronicles of Tilehouse Street Baptist Church, 1669-1969.* London, Tonbridge: Whitefriars P., 1969.

Farrer, K.T.H. *William Carey: missionary and botanist.* Kew, Victoria: Carey Baptist Grammar School, 2005.

Fath, S. *Les Baptistes en France (1810-1950): faits, dates et documents.* Cléon d'Andran: Excelsis, 2002.

Fereday L.A. *The story of Falmouth Baptists: with some account of Cornish Baptist beginnings.* London: Carey Kingsgate Press, [1950].

Field, C.D. Preserving Zion: the anatomy of Protestant Nonconformist archives in Great Britain and Ireland. *Archives,* xxxiii(118), April 2008, pp. 14-51.

Fisher, J.S. *Impelled by faith: a short history of the Baptists in Scotland.* Stirling: Scottish Baptist History Project, 1996.

Fisher, J.S. *People of the Meeting House: tales of a church in Luton.* [Luton?: s.n., 1976?]

Freeman, C.W. et al. *Baptist roots: a reader in the theology of a Christian people.* Valley Forge: Judson Press, c1999.

Gandy, M. *Basic facts about English nonconformity for family historians.* Birmingham: Federation of Family History Societies, 1998.

Gandy, M. *Tracing nonconformist ancestors.* Richmond: Public Record Office , 2001.

Garrett, J.L. *Baptist theology: a four-century study. Macon, Ga.:* Mercer University Press, 2009.

Gibbins, H.D. *The history and development of the Baptist churches in Middlesborough.* [Middlesborough?]: the author, 1994.

Gill, A. *A bibliography of Baptist writings on Baptism, 1900-1968.* Rüschlikon-Zürich: Baptist Theological Seminary, 1969.

Godfrey, J.R. *Historic memorials of Barton & Melbourne General Baptist churches: including their numerous offshoots since 1760; biographical sketches of the leading ministers and laymen; together with portraits and other illustrations.* Leicester: Buck, Winks and Son, 1891.

Gould, G.P. *The Baptist College at Regent's Park: a centenary record.* London: Kingsgate P., 1910.

Grams, R.G. and Parushev, P.R. (eds.) *Towards an understanding of European Baptist identity: listening to the Churches in Armenia, Bulgaria, Central Asia, Moldova, North Caucasus, Omsk and Poland;* mapping Baptistic identity. Praha: International Baptist Theological Seminary of the European Baptist Federation, 2006.

Greasley, S. *The Baptists of Derbyshire: 1650-1914.* Ilkeston: Moorley's Print & publishing, c2007.

Greaves, R.L. & Zaller, R. (eds.) *Biographical Dictionary of British radicals in the seventeenth century.* 3 vols. Brighton: Harvester Press, 1982-4.

Green, B. *Crossing the boundaries: a history of the European Baptist Federation.* Didcot: Baptist Historical Society, 1999.

Green, B. *European Baptists and the Third Reich.* (Forthcoming). Baptist Historical Society, 2009.

Green, B. *Tomorrow's man: a biography of James Henry Rushbrooke.* Didcot: Baptist Historical Society, c1997.

Gregory, F. and Willett, P. *Deacon's dissenters raise the cross: the history, origin & memoirs of Cross Hills Baptist Church.* Coalville, Leics.: Catamount, 1998.

Griffin-Allwood, P.G.A., et al. *Baptists in Canada 1760-1990: a bibliography of selected printed resources in English.* Hantsport, N.S.: Lancelot Press, 1989.

Hall, C. *Civilising subjects: metropole and colony in the English imagination, 1830-1867.* Oxford: Polity Press, 2002.

Hambleton, M.G. *A sweet and hopeful people: the story of Abingdon Baptist Church 1649-2000.* Abingdon: the author, 2000.

Harrison, F.M.W. *It all began here: the story of the East Midland Baptist Association.* London: East Midlands Baptist Association, c1986.

Hayden, E.W. *A centennial history of Spurgeon's Tabernacle.* London: Clifford Frost, 1962. Reprinted with an additional chapter and bibliographical appendices. Pasadena, Tex: Pilgrim Publications, 1971.

Hayden, R. (ed.) *Baptist Union documents, 1948-1977.* London: Baptist Historical Society, 1980.

Hayden, R. *Continuity and change: evangelical Calvinism among eighteenth-century Baptist ministers trained at Bristol Academy, 1690-1791.* Chipping Norton: Nigel Lynn for Roger Hayden and the Baptist Historical Society, 2006.

Hayden, R. *English Baptist history and heritage.* 2nd ed. Didcot: Baptist Union of Great Britain, 2005.

Hayden, R. (ed.) *The records of a church of Christ in Bristol, 1640-1687.* Gateshead: Bristol Record Society, 1974.

Haykin, M.A.G. (ed.) *The British Particular Baptists, 1638-1910.* 3 v. Springfield, MO: Particular Baptist Press, c1998-2003.

Hebden, S. *Baptismal regeneration disproved; the scripture account of the nature of regeneration explained; ...* London printed for R. Hett and J. Oswald, 1741.

Helwys, T. *A short declaration of the mistery of iniquity.* [Amsterdam?: s.n.], Anno 1612. Facsimile reprint as *The mistery of iniquity.* London: Kingsgate Press for the Baptist Historical Society, 1935.

Helwys, T. *A short declaration of the mystery of iniquity*; edited by Richard Groves. Macon, Ga.: Mercer University Press, c1998.

Hopkins, M. *Nonconformity's romantic generation: evangelical and liberal theologies in Victorian England.* Milton Keynes: Paternoster, 2004.

Howard, K.W.H. 'Index Nominum Ivimiana'. [unpublished] 1981.

Hudson-Reed, S. ed. *Together for a century: the history of the Baptist Union of South Africa, 1877-1977.* Pietermaritzburg: S.A. Baptist Historical Society, [1977].

Index to notable Baptists, whose careers began within the British Empire before 1850. *Transactions of the Baptist Historical Society*, 7, 1920-21, p. 182-239. [Whitley, W.T.] Notable Baptists: Additions and corrections to the list in Volume VII. *Baptist Quarterly*, (New series) 1, 1922-23, p. 286-288.

Ivimey, J. *A history of the English Baptists.* 4 v. London: Printed for the author , 1811-30.

James, J.S. *Hanes y Bedyddwyr yn Nghymru.* 4 v. Caerfyrddin: Seren Cymru, 1896-1907.

Jeal, R. *Maidstone Baptist Church, 1834-1984.* [Maidstone: Maidstone Baptist Church, 1984?]
Johnson, C.J. *Encounter in London: the story of the London Baptist Association, 1865-1965.* London: Carey Kingsgate Press, 1965.

Johnson, D.A. *The changing shape of English nonconformity, 1825-1925*. New York, Oxford: Oxford University Press, 1999.

Jones, A.D. *Twenty golden candlesticks revisited: Wiltshire Baptist history 1890-2005*. Published by the author, 2008.

Jones, E.K. *The Baptists of Wales and ministerial education: also the nonconformist theological colleges of Wales*. Wrexham: Hughes, 1902.

Jones, G. *The descent of Dissent: a guide to the Nonconformist records at the Leicestershire Record Office*. Leicester: Leicestershire Museums, Arts and Record Service, 1989.

Jones, J.A. (ed.) *Bunhill memorials: sacred reminiscences of three hundred ministers and other persons of note, who are buried in Bunhill Fields, of every denomination* ... London: James Paul, 1849.

Jones, K.G. and Randall, I.M. (eds.) *Counter-cultural communities: Baptistic life in twentieth-century Europe*. Milton Keynes: Paternoster, 2008.

Jordan, E.K.H. *The church at the Hay Well: how Baptists came to Malvern*. Malvern: Malvern Baptist Church, 1987.

Kingdon, D.P. *Bibliography of books on Baptist history*. [Belfast: the author, c1970]

Kinghorn, J. *The life and works of Joseph Kinghorn*; edited by Terry Wolever. 2 v. (of ultimate 4 v.) Springfield, MO: Particular Baptist Press, 1995- .

Klaiber, A.J. *The story of the Suffolk Baptists*. London: Kingsgate Press, [1931]

Kreitzer, L.J. *'Seditious Sectaryes': the Baptist Conventiclers of Oxford 1641-1691*. Milton Keynes: Paternoster, 2006.

Langley, A.S. Baptist ministers in England about 1750 A.D. *Transactions of the Baptist Historical Society*, vol. 6, 1918-19, pp. 138-162.

Langley, A.S. *Birmingham Baptists, past and present: prepared for the West Midland Baptist Association*. London: Kingsgate Press, [1939].

Leonard, Bill J. *Baptist ways: a history*. Valley Forge, PA: Judson Press, 2003.

Leonard, Bill J. *Baptists in America*. New York: Columbia University Press, c2005.

Lewis, D.M. (ed.) *The Blackwell dictionary of evangelical biography: 1730-1860*. Oxford: Blackwell, 1995.

Light, A.W. *Bunhill Fields: written in honour and to the memory of the many saints of God whose bodies rest in this old London cemetery*. 2 v. London: Farncombe, 1913, 1933. (Reprinted in one volume in 2003 by Tentmaker Publications.)

Livingstone, E.A. (ed.) *The concise Oxford dictionary of the Christian church*. Rev. 2nd ed. Oxford University Press, 2006.

Lord, F.T. *Baptist world fellowship: a short history of the Baptist World Alliance*. *London: Carey Kingsgate Press, [1955]*.

Lovegrove, D.W. *Established church, sectarian people: itinerancy and the transformation of English dissent, 1780-1830*. Cambridge: Cambridge University Press, 1988.

Lumpkin, W.L. *Baptist confessions of faith*. Chicago: Judson Press, [1959].

Manley, K. *'Redeeming love proclaim': John Rippon and the Baptists*. Carlisle: Paternoster, 2004.

Manley, K.R. *From Woolloomooloo to 'eternity': a history of Australian Baptists*. 2 v. Milton Keynes: Paternoster, 2006.

Maselli, D. *Storia dei Battisti italiani: 1873-1923*. Torino: Claudiana, 2003.

Matthews, A.G. *Calamy revised: being a revision of Edmund Calamy's Account of the ministers and others ejected and silenced 1660-2*. Oxford: Clarendon Press, 1934 (rev. 1988)

Matthews, A.G. *Walker revised, being a revision of John Walker's Sufferings of the clergy during the Grand Rebellion 1642-60*. Oxford: Clarendon Press, 1948 (rev. 1988).

Matthews, D.H. *From Abergavenny to Cardiff: history of the South Wales Baptist College (1806-2006)*. Abertawe [Swansea] : Gwasg Ilston, 2007.

McBeth, H.L. *The Baptist heritage*. Nashville, Tenn.: Broadman Press, c1987.

McBeth, L. *A sourcebook for Baptist heritage*. Nashville, Tenn.: Broadman Press, 1990.

McGlothlin, W.J. *Baptist confessions of faith*. Philadelphia: American Baptists Publication Society, 1911.

McIntyre, W.E. *Baptist authors: a manual of bibliography, 1500-1914*. [Number 1(-3); A(-Day)] 3 pts. in 1 v. Montreal, Toronto: Industrial and Educational Press, [1914].

McLaughlin, E. *Nonconformist ancestors*. Haddenham: Varneys Press, 1995.

McLoughlin, W.G. *New England Dissent, 1630-1833: the Baptists and the separation of church and state.* 2 v. Cambridge, Mass.: Harvard University Press, 1971.

McLoughlin, W.G. *Soul liberty: the Baptists' struggle in New England, 1630-1833.* Hanover, London: University Press of New England for Brown University Press, c1991.

Mitchell, S. *Not disobedient: a history of United Baptist Church, Leicester, including Harvey Lane 1760-1845, Belvoir Street 1845-1940, and Charles Street 1831-1940. [A brief history of] United Baptist Church 1940-1983; Graham Lee.* [Leicester: S. Mitchell], c1984.

Moon, N. S. *Education for ministry: Bristol Baptist College 1679-1979*. Bristol: Bristol Baptist College, 1979.

Mullett, M.A. *Sources for the history of English Nonconformity, 1660-1830.* [London]: British Records Association, 1991.

Murch, J. *A history of the Presbyterian and General Baptist churches in the West of England: with memoirs of some of their pastors.* London: Hunter, 1835.

Murray, D.B. *Scottish Baptist College: centenary history 1894-1994.* Glasgow: Scottish Baptist College, 1994.

Naylor, P. *Picking up a pin for the Lord: English Particular Baptists from 1688 to the early nineteenth century.* London: Grace Pubns., 1992.

Naylor, P. *Calvinism, Communion and the Baptists: a study of English Calvinistic Baptists from the late 1600s to the early 1800s.* Carlisle: Paternoster Press, 2003.

Neal, D. *The history of the Puritans, or, Protestant non-conformists, ... with an account of their principles...* A new ed., revised, corrected, and enlarged by Joshua Toulmin. 5 v. Bath, London, Bristol: 1793-1797.

Neil, D.F. *The Baptists of North East England 1650-2000.* Houghton-le-Spring: the author, 2006.

Nicholls, M. *Lights to the world: a history of Spurgeon's College 1856-1992.* Harpenden: in association with Nuprint, 1994.

Nicholson, H.M. *Authentic records relating to the Christian church now meeting in George Street and Mutley Chapels, Plymouth, 1640-1870.* London: Elliot Stock, [1870?].

Noll, M.A. *The rise of evangelicalism: the age of Edwards, Whitefield and the Wesleys.* Nottingham: Inter-Varsity Press, 2004.

Nonconformist congregations in Great Britain: a list of histories and other material in Dr. Williams's Library. London: Dr. Williams's Trust, 1973.

Nonconformist records: a brief introduction. Kingston upon Thames: Surrey Record Office, c1988.

Northamptonshire Association. *Qualifications for church fellowship: the circular letter ... , 1800.*

Nuttall, G.F. *Studies in English dissent.* Weston Rhyn, Shropshire: Quinta Press, 2002.

Nuttall, G.F. 'Assembly and Association in Dissent, 1689-1831', in *Councils and assemblies: papers read at the ... meeting of the Ecclesiastical History Society*; ed. G.J. Cuming and Derek Baker. Cambridge: University Press, 1971. (*Studies in church history*, 7)

Oddie, G. A. *Imagined Hinduism: British Protestant missionary constructions of Hinduism, 1793-1900.*

Oliver, R.W. *History of the English Calvinistic Baptists 1771-1892: from John Gill to C.H. Spurgeon.* Edinburgh: Banner of Truth Trust, 2006.

Overend, F. *History of the Ebenezer Baptist Church, Bacup. Together with an historical account of the "Church of Christ in Rossendale", based on the Mitchel and Crosley letters, hitherto unpublished.* London: Kingsgate Press, 1912.

Palgrave-Moore, P. *Understanding the history and records of nonconformity.* 2nd ed. [Norwich]: Elvery Dowers, 1988.

Park, K. *Non-conformist records.* Mountain Ash: Knowledge Base Publications, 1995.

Paul, S.F. *Further history of the Gospel Standard Baptists.* 6 v. [Brighton: the author, vol. 6 Gospel Standard Baptist Trust Ltd.], 1951-1969.

Payne, E.A. *The Baptist Union: a short history.* London: Carey Kingsgate Press, 1959, c1958.

Payne, E.A. *The Baptists of Berkshire through three centuries.* London: Carey Kingsgate Press, [1951].

Payne, E.A. *The fellowship of believers: Baptist thought and practice yesterday and today.* Enl. ed. London: Carey Kingsgate Press, 1952.

Payne, E.A. *The first generation: early leaders of the Baptist Missionary Society in England and India.* London: Carey Press, [1936?].

Payne, E.A. *The Free Church tradition in the life of England.* 3rd ed. rev. London: SCM Press, [1951].

Payne, E.A. *The great succession: leaders of the Baptist Missionary Society during the nineteenth century.* 2nd ed. London: Carey Press, 1946.

Penner, P.F. (ed.) *Ethnic churches in Europe: a Baptist response.* Schwarzenfeld: Neufeld, 2006.

Pierard, R.V. (ed.) *Baptists together in Christ, 1905-2005: a hundred-year history of the Baptist World Alliance.* Falls Church, Va.: Baptist World Alliance, c2005.

Pollard, A.W. & Redgrave, G.R. *A short-title catalogue of books printed in England, Scotland, & Ireland and of English books printed abroad 1475-1640.* 2nd ed. rev. & enl. 3 v. London: The Bibliographical Society, 1986-91.

Price, S.J. *Upton: the story of one hundred and fifty years 1785-1935.* London: Carey Press, 1935.

Protestant Nonconformist texts. 4 v. Aldershot: Ashgate, 2006 - 2007.

Randall, I.M. *Communities of conviction: Baptist beginnings in Europe.* [Prague: European Baptist Federation, Projected date May 2009].

Randall, I.M. *The English Baptists of the twentieth century.* Didcot: Baptist Historical Society, 2005.

Randall, I.M. *A school of the prophets: 150 years of Spurgeon's College.* London: Spurgeon's College, 2005.

Randall, I.M. and Cross, A.R. (eds.) *Baptists and mission: papers from the Fourth International Conference on Baptist Studies.* Milton Keynes: Paternoster, 2007.

Randall, I.M., Pilli, T. and Cross, A.R. (eds.) *Baptist identities: international studies from the seventeenth to the twentieth century.* Milton Keynes: Paternoster, 2006.

Rippon, J. *The Baptist annual register for 1790 [– 1802], including sketches of the state of religion among different denominations of good men at home and abroad.* 4 v. [London: 1792-1802.]

Roberts, R.P. *Continuity and change: London Calvinistic Baptists and the Evangelical Revival, 1760-1820.* Wheaton, Ill.: Richard Owen Roberts, c1989.

Roxburgh, W. *Hortus Bengalensis.* Serampore: The Mission Press, 1814.

Rushbrooke, J.H. *The Baptist movement in the continent of Europe.* Rev.ed. London: Carey Press, 1923.

Ruston, A. *My ancestors were English Presbyterians or Unitarians: how can I find out more about them?* 2nd ed. London: Society of Genealogists, 2001.

Ruston, A. *Obituaries and marriages of dissenting ministers in the Gentleman's Magazine in the 18th century*, extracted and annotated by Alan Ruston. Watford: Alan Ruston, 1996.

Ruston, A.R. *Nonconformity in Hertfordshire: a guide to sources for family and local historians*. Barnet: Hertfordshire Family History Society, 2005.

Sell, A.P.F. and Cross, A.R. (eds.) *Protestant nonconformity in the twentieth century*. Carlisle: Paternoster, 2003.

Sell, A.P.F. *Nonconformist theology in the twentieth century*. Carlisle: Paternoster Press, 2006.

Shakespeare, J.H. *Baptist and Congregational pioneers*. [2nd ed.] London: National Council of Evangelical Free Churches, [1907].

Shankland, T. *Shankland ar ddiwygwyr Cymru*. [s.l.: Seren Gomer, 1900-1904.]

Shepherd, P. *The making of a modern denomination: John Howard Shakespeare and the English Baptists 1894-1924*. Carlisle: Paternoster, 2001.

Shepherd, P. *The making of a northern Baptist college*. [Manchester]: Northern Baptist College, 2004.

Shorney, D. *Protestant nonconformity and Roman Catholicism: a guide to sources in the Public Record Office*. London: PRO Publications, 1996.

Smyth, J. *The works of John Smyth, Fellow of Christ's College, 1594-8*. Tercentenary ed., with notes and biography by W.T. Whitley. Cambridge: Cambridge University Press for the Baptist Historical Society, 1915.

Southern Baptist Historical Library and Archives. *Guide to microfilm of Baptist Missionary Society Archives, London, England, 1792-1914*. Microfilm publication no. 5350. Nashville, Te., [198-?]

Spyvee, H. *Colchester Baptist Church - the first 300 years, 1689-1989: now worshipping at Eld Lane and Blackheath*. Colchester: Colchester Baptist Church, 1989.

Stanley, B. *The history of the Baptist Missionary Society, 1792-1992*. Edinburgh: T&T Clark, 1992.

Starr, E.C. *A Baptist bibliography. being a register of printed material by and about Baptists; including works written against the Baptists.* 25 v. Philadelphia: Judson Press for the Samuel Colgate Baptist Historical Collection, Colgate University, 1947-76.

Steel, D.J. *Sources for nonconformist genealogy and family history.* London: Society of Genealogists, 1973.

Stell, C. *An inventory of nonconformist chapels and meeting-houses in central England.* London: H.M.S.O., 1986.

Stell, C. *An inventory of nonconformist chapels and meeting-houses in south-west England.* London: H.M.S.O., 1991.

Stell, C. *An inventory of nonconformist chapels and meeting-houses in the north of England.* London: H.M.S.O., 1994.

Stell, C. *An inventory of nonconformist chapels and meeting-houses in Eastern England.* Swindon: English Heritage, 2002.

Stock, J. *History of the Baptised Independent and Congregational Church, meeting in Salendine Nook chapel, Huddersfield.* London: Elliot Stock, [187-].

[Stock, P.] *Foundations: [a history of Salendine Nook Baptist Chapel, Huddersfield].* Halifax: Edward Mortimer, 1933.

Strübind, A. *Die unfreie Freikirche: der Bund der Baptistengemeinden im "Dritten Reich".* Neukirchen-Vluyn: Neukirchener, c1991.

Sutherland, M. (ed.) *Baptists in colonial New Zealand: documents illustrating Baptist life and development.* Auckland: New Zealand Baptist Research and Historical Society, 2002.

Sutton, J. *A Matter of Conviction: A History of Southern Baptist Engagement with the Culture.* Nashville: B&H Publishing, 2008.

Swaine, S.A. *Faithful men: or, memorials of Bristol Baptist College, and some of its most distinguished alumni.* London: Alexander & Shepheard, 1884.

Talbot, B.R. *The search for a common identity: the origins of the Baptist Union of Scotland 1800-1870.* Carlisle: Paternoster, 2003.

Taylor, A. *The history of the English General Baptists: in two parts.* 2 v. London: Printed for the author, 1818.

Thomas, J. *A history of the Baptist Association in Wales, from the year 1650, to the year 1790.* London: sold by Messrs. Dilly, Button, and Thomas, ... 1795.

Thomas, J. *Hanes y Bedyddwyr, ymhlith y Cymry,: o amser yr Apostolion, hyd y flwyddyn hon: yn ddwy ran* ... Caerfyrddin: Argraphwyd, dros yr awdwr, gan John Ross, 1778.

Thompson, D.M. (ed.) *Nonconformity in the nineteenth century.* London: Routledge & Kegan Paul, 1972.

Thompson, J. *Century of grace: the Baptist Union of Ireland; a short history, 1895-1995.* Belfast: Baptist Union of Ireland, 1995.

Thompson, P.E. and Cross, A.R. (eds.): *Recycling the past or researching history?: studies in Baptist historiography and myths.* Milton Keynes: Paternoster, 2005.

Thomson, R.W. *Heroes of the Baptist Church.* London: Kingsgate Press, 1937.

Tonson, P. *A handful of grain: the centenary history of the Baptist Union of N.Z.* 4 v. Wellington, N.Z.: N.Z. Baptist Historical Society for the Baptist Union of New Zealand, [1982]-1984.

Torbet, R.G. *A history of the Baptists.* Philadelphia: Judson Press, 1950. Rev. 1st British ed. London: Carey Kingsgate Press, 1966. 3rd ed. Valley Forge: Judson Press, 1963, 1975.

Tracing your family history in Hertfordshire. Hatfield: Hertfordshire Pubns. for HALS, 2003.

Underhill, E.B. (ed.) *Confessions of faith and other public documents illustrative of the history of the Baptist Churches of England in the 17th century.* London: Haddon Brothers for the Hanserd Knollys Society, 1854.

Underhill, E.B. (ed.) *A martyrology of the churches of Christ, commonly called Baptists, during the era of the Reformation*; translated from the Dutch of T.J. van Braght. London: J. Haddon and Son for the Hanserd Knollys Society, 1850-1853.

Underhill, E.B. (ed.) *Records of the churches of Christ, gathered at Fenstanton, Warboys, and Hexham, 1644-1720.* London: Hanserd Knollys Society, 1854.

Underhill, E.B. (ed.) *The bloudy tenent of persecution for cause of conscience discussed: and Mr Cotton's letter examined and answered by Roger Williams.* London: J. Haddon for the Hanserd Knollys Society, 1848.

Underhill, E.B. (ed.) *Tracts on liberty of conscience and persecution, 1614-1661.* London: J. Haddon for the Hanserd Knollys Society, 1846.

Underhill, E.B., (ed.) *The records of a church of Christ meeting in Broadmead, Bristol, 1640-1687.* London: J. Haddon for the Hanserd Knollys Society, 1847.

Underwood, A.C. *A history of the English Baptists.* London: Baptist Union Publ. Dept., 1947.

Ward, G. *Sources for researching Nonconformists in Northamptonshire.* [Northampton]: Northamptonshire Family History Society, 2004.

Wardin, A.W. (ed.) *Baptists around the world: a comprehensive handbook.* Nashville, TN: Broadman & Holman, 1995.

Wardin, A.W. *The twelve Baptist tribes in the United States: a historical and statistical analysis.* Atlanta, Ga.: Baptist History and Heritage Society; Nashville, Tenn.: Fields Publishing Inc.; 2007.

Watts, M.R. *The dissenters.* Oxford: Clarendon Press, c1978-95.

West Midlands Baptist Association. *Records of an old association: being a memorial volume of the 250th anniversary of the Midland, now the West Midland, Baptist Association, formed in Warwick, May 3rd, 1655*; [edited by J.M. Gwynne Owen]. [Birmingham: Allday, 1905.]

West-Riding of Yorkshire Association of Baptist churches. *A brief historical account of the churches in the Association. The Circular letter ... , 1842;...* Leeds: printed by John Heaton, 1842.

Whelan, T. 'A chronological calendar of Baptist autographs at the John Rylands University Library of Manchester, 1741-1907,' *Baptist Quarterly,* 42(8), Oct. 2008, p. 577-612.

Whelan, T. *Baptist autographs at the John Rylands University Library of Manchester, 1741-1845.* (Forthcoming. Macon, Ga.: Mercer University Press, 2009.)

White, B.R. *The English Baptists of the seventeenth century.* Rev. enl. ed. Didcot: Baptist Historical Society, c1996.

White, B.R.(ed.) *Association records of the Particular Baptists of England, Wales and Ireland to 1660.* 3 parts + Index. London: Baptist Historical Society, 1971-4.

Whitley, W.T. *A Baptist bibliography: being a register of the chief materials for Baptist history, whether in manuscript or in print, preserved in Great Britain, Ireland and the Colonies [1526-1837].* 2 v. London: Kingsgate Press, 1916-1922. Reprint, 2 v. in 1. Hildesheim, New York: G. Olms, 1984.

Whitley, W.T. *The Baptists of London, 1612-1928: their fellowship, their expansion, with notes on their 850 churches.* London: Kingsgate Press, [1928?].

Whitley, W.T. *Baptists of North-West England: 1649-1913.* London, Preston: Kingsgate, Toulmin, for the Lancashire & Cheshire Association, 1913.

Whitley, W.T. *A history of British Baptists.* 2nd rev ed. London: Kingsgate, 1932.

Whitley, W.T. (ed.) *Minutes of the General Assembly of the General Baptist churches in England: with kindred records.* London: Kingsgate Press for the Baptist Historical Society, [1909]-1910.

Williams, R. *The bloudy tenant of persecution for cause of conscience;* ed. Richard Groves; historical intro. Edwin S. Gaustad. Macon, Ga.: Mercer University Press, [200-?]

Wilson, W. *The history and antiquities of dissenting churches and meeting houses in London, Westminster and Southwark, including the lives of their ministers.* 4 v. London: Printed for the author; [various booksellers] 1808-[14].

Wing, D.G. *Short-title catalogue of books printed in England, Scotland, Ireland, Wales and British America, and of English books printed in other countries, 1641-1700.* 3 v. New York, 1945-51. 2nd ed. rev. and enl. 4 v. New York: Modern Language Association of America, 1982-1998.

Witard, D. *Bibles in barrels: a history of Essex Baptists.* [Colchester]: Essex Baptist Association, [1962].

Wood, J.H. *A condensed history of the General Baptists of the New Connexion, preceded by historical sketches of the early Baptists.* London: Simpkin, Marshall; Leicester: Winks, 1847.

Wright, C.T. Hagberg. *Subject-index of the London Library.* Vol.1. London: Williams & Norgate, 1909. Vols.2-4, London Library. Additions, 1909-22,1923-38,1938-53. London, 1923, 1938, 1955.

Wright, S. *The early English Baptists, 1603-1649.* Woodbridge: Boydell Press, 2006.

Yorkshire Baptist Association. *The Baptists of Yorkshire: being the centenary memorial volume of the Yorkshire Baptist Association.* Bradford, London: Byles, Kingsgate, 1912.

Yuille, G. (ed.) *History of the Baptists in Scotland from pre-Reformation times.* Glasgow: Baptist Union of Scotland, [1926].